STOLEN
CHARLESTON

STOLEN
CHARLESTON

THE
SPOILS
OF
WAR

J. GRAHAME LONG

Charleston | London

THE
History
PRESS

Published by The History Press
Charleston, SC 29403
www.historypress.net

First published 2014

Manufactured in the United States

ISBN 978.1.62619.096.2

Library of Congress CIP data applied for.

For Lissa

CONTENTS

Acknowledgements   9

I. Elegance Lost   11
II. A (Once) Good Life   25
III. Defilers at the Door   35
IV. (Im)Proper Burials   53
V. The Pursuit of Provisions   71
VI. Trouble from Home   85
VII. Losing Faith   103
VIII. Lost and Found   121

Notes   139
Bibliography   151
Index   167
About the Author   175

Acknowledgements

While there are some things that can be accomplished alone and unaided, this book is in no way one of them. I wish to express my tremendous thanks to the following for their help and support:

John Young, assistant director, the Powder Magazine; Frank Justice; Lauren Northup, museum manager, Historic Charleston Foundation; Mary Edna Sullivan, curator, Middleton Place Foundation; Phillip Middleton; Bru Izard; Lee Manigault; Louisa Montgomery; Keith Leonard; Robin Rice; Matt and Susan Verdery; W.B. Chisolm Leonard, parish administrator, St. Philip's Episcopal Church; Brain Fahay, archivist, Catholic Diocese of Charleston; Cheralaine Dougherty, parish administrator, Christ Church; Charlotte Crabtree; Reverend Daniel Massie, pastor and head of staff, First (Scots) Presbyterian Church; Jeff Ball; Robert Ball Jr.; Gillian Bagley, parish administrator, Church of the Good Shepherd; Lieutenant Charles Fazio, curator, Ancient and Honorable Artillery Company; the MacMeekin family; and Don Horres, executive director, Mount Pleasant Presbyterian Church.

Of course, the outstanding and dedicated staff at the Charleston Museum, especially director Carl Borick, graphic designer and photographer Sean Money and archivist and collections manager Jennifer McCormick. As always, to my family for their enthusiasm, faith and extreme patience.

I

Elegance Lost

On January 24, 1945, a package arrived with the daily mail at the Christ Church on Rutledge Avenue and immediately caught the eye of Reverend Edmund Coe. While not unusual for a busy church, this particular Illinois-postmarked parcel delivery was eagerly anticipated. Within the neatly packed box was a large coin-silver vessel with a small lamb finial on the hinged top. The maker's mark on the bottom denoted the piece's Charleston artisan, John Ewan, a silversmith and jeweler from 1823 to 1852. Although Reverend Coe had carried on some previous correspondence with the parcel sender, nothing could have prepared him for this moment. After eighty years, the Christ Church flagon was home.[1]

In her first communication with Reverend Coe some weeks earlier, Mrs. Bonnie McArty had explained how she and her family made their embarrassing discovery. "We were doing some work on our home," she wrote, "and came across [the flagon] and thought I would shine it up. Well, that is the first we knew it had any inscription on it." Believing the piece not rightfully theirs, McArty's letter further made an earnest plea to Reverend Coe, hoping he and the rest of the church might forgive her uncle, Frank Blaine, a Union infantryman in Charleston after the 1865 Confederate evacuation. It seemed that Blaine, "a very young boy" at the time, stole the flagon from a deserted church and "brought it home." Only long after his death had it been discovered by his descendants, who were now determined to set things right and return the ill-gotten war prize after so many years.[2]

Above: Coin-silver flagon (marked by Charleston silversmith John Ewan circa 1840) taken from Christ Church's Rutledge Avenue location in 1865 and returned to Charleston in 1945. *Courtesy of the Church of the Good Shepherd, Charleston; photo by Keith Leonard.*

Opposite: *Searching for Arms* by Adalbert John Volck, circa 1890. *Library of Congress.*

As surprising as it may be that one of Charleston's artifacts actually made it home, the sheer fact that it went missing during wartime is anything but. Charleston has scarcely been a stranger to hardship. Devastation has seemingly always been close at hand. Among various calamities, Charleston is the rare American city that had two wars fought on its own soil, each resulting in heavy artillery sieges and subsequent enemy occupations. Expectedly, alongside these intrusions arrived soldierly lawlessness on a grand scale.

Practically everyone in Charleston seems to have at least one old family tale involving run-ins with the enemy and the heirlooms they took away. Even today, the American Revolution and Civil War together are believed by many to be "the single greatest cause for the disappearance of old pieces." Based solely on these oral histories, then, it would appear that neither church, home nor citizen was immune to the incomparable losses brought by war's encroachment on the Charleston home front.[3]

When examined from a historical perspective, wartime plundering is not exactly hard to find among city and state records. In fact, it is hard—nigh impossible—to name any war in all of human history that has occurred without some form of soldierly pillaging once within the enemy home front. For that reason, then, was it not bound to happen in Charleston as a mere accompanying element of warfare? Indeed, wartime raiding and plundering is as old as even the most basic concept of conquest. "To the victor go the spoils!" proclaimed Senator William L. Macy in 1832, an utterance that still finds adherents in any number of today's war-riddled locales. Allusions in classical literature are abundant as well. Tolstoy, Hugo and Shakespeare each consistently referred to episodes outside of normal warfare, where looting and pillaging were considered a right. Mental images of historical combat victories from every era bring about evocations of confiscated, if not illicitly obtained, rewards. Indeed, how boring classical pirate lore would be if pillage and plunder were nonissues![4]

Looking back further among the ancients, pillage was not so much a perquisite as it was an actual strategy by which vanquishers further degraded their enemies. So what if an opponent was defeated on the battle front? They must be soundly crushed on the home front as well by having their possessions or perhaps even themselves seized as war booty. As Isaiah attests in the Old Testament, "This is a people plundered and looted, all of them trapped…They have become plunder." As time marched on, of course, the universally understood notion of wartime spoils took on a somewhat newer principle—or at least one with a more important cultural usage. That is, merchandise and other valuables became necessary. For example, Genghis Khan, perhaps the greatest war looter the world has ever known, not only acquired plunder but also controlled it, masterfully redistributing it to his raiders as collective income and thus further motivating his troops by making "great promises and glowing representations…in respect to the booty to be obtained."[5]

Luckily, the more recent militaries of the eighteenth and nineteenth centuries did not set out to mindlessly despoil their foes. In 1806, in fact, the ninth U.S. Congress directly addressed the issue, making it deathly clear that within the ranks, any ill-obtained goods would not be tolerated. From the Articles of War Chapter 20, Article 52: "Any Officer, or soldier, who shall misbehave himself before the enemy…to plunder and pillage, every such offender, being duly convicted thereof, shall suffer death, or such other punishment as shall be ordered."[6]

Despite these potentially dire consequences, however, willful theft of personal property had been and would continue to be an unfortunate, albeit rather common, derivative of Charleston-centric military conflict, and this "predatory warfare," though certainly not condoned, encouraged or even legal, was in most instances impossible to prevent. In speaking of his officers in 1866, Colonel C.W.H. Davis of the 104th Pennsylvania Regiment noted, "Some of them sent north pianos, elegant furniture, silverware, books, pictures, etc. to adorn their New England homes." Worse still, press correspondent Captain David P. Conyngham, while traveling through the Carolinas with General William Sherman, recorded several chilling acts perpetrated by his Union comrades, one of whom admitted to killing civilians: "As for the wholesale burnings, pillage and devastation committed in South Carolina, magnify all [that was done] of Georgia some fifty-fold, and then throw in an occasional murder…and you have a pretty good idea of the whole thing."[7]

Naturally, there are myriad explanations and even a few apologists for it all, but the reasoning and psychology behind such instances appear simple enough: delayed pay, involuntary conscription or just general mob mentality. Regardless of the motivating factors, no matter how reactionary, the ultimate result was a general feeling that if for no other reason, the soldiers had simply earned it. Plunder was more than mere compensation, and within the natural thinking of many, it was a justifiable, if not due, reward. Human nature itself pragmatically consigns war looting to the realm of retribution, usually producing catastrophic results for those vanquished. Like Frank Blaine, these were young, impressionable, barely of-age lads risking life and limb for a cause. To survive and earn a victory under such violent and certainly bloody circumstances was a massive relief. As a result, and with the realization of getting to live another day, there was certainly ample motive for a celebration—even if it were one bent on revenge. Charlestonian Dr. David Ramsay reflected on this powerful feeling of entitlement among the redcoats during their occupation of the city:

> *The common soldiers, from their sufferings and services…conceived themselves entitled to a licensed plunder of the town. That their murmurings might be soothed, the officers connived at their reimbursing themselves for their fatigues and dangers at the expense of the citizens…The officers, privates, and followers of the royal army, were generally more intent on amassing fortunes by plunder and rapine than in promoting a re-union of the dissevered members of the empire…From an army abounding with such unworthy characters, and stationed among a people whom they hated as rebels…it was not reasonable to expect that winning behavior which was necessary to conciliate the affection of the revolted States.*[8]

During the Civil War, several Union generals and other commanding officers, to their credit, did their utmost to stave off the plundering of civilians. Thinking progressively after nearly one full year of combat, Sherman put forth Order No. 7 in March 1862, declaring that any officer or soldier caught pillaging, plundering or allowing either would "surely be punished" and went so far as to cite the aforementioned congressional mandates of 1806 allowing the death penalty for such transgressions. However, as the war dragged on beyond what practically everyone initially expected, his requests became harder and harder to obey—even by his own staff, some of whom had a real knack for twisting their commander's words. "Soldiers don't steal, they confiscate" was what one self-proclaimed "Northern Vandal" told Reverend and Mrs. Trapier as he took the rings off the couple's fingers.[9]

Sherman's colleagues fared no better. Though Union general Quincy A. Gillmore had once been called "the most atrocious house-burner as yet unhung in the wide universe," he still made earnest attempts to stop unbridled Charleston plundering in 1865. He wrote to General John P. Hatch: "I hear on all sides very discouraging accounts of the state of affairs in Charleston; that no restraint is put upon the soldiers; that they pilfer and rob houses at pleasure; that large quantities of furniture, paintings, statuary, mirrors, etc. have mysteriously disappeared…and that matters are generally at sixes and sevens." Gillmore ultimately issued three separate orders to stop looting Charleston—his third specifically ordering officers to return "silver, furniture, pianos, organs, pictures, and works of art." None of it was.[10]

Of course, no matter what the generals might have said, none of them could be everywhere at once, let alone keep a close eye on every soldier all the time. Consequently, once Federal forces occupied the state in 1865, a general riving of both urban and rural properties was nearly inevitable. The *Columbia Phoenix* newspaper, for example, reported on March 23 that upward of 1,200 pocket watches were "transferred from the pockets of their owners" into Yankee haversacks. Persistent stories like these, be they truth or fabrication, led Benjamin Huger of Charleston to write that, as far as he was concerned, "Napoleon never did anything that approached it!"[11]

Unquestionably, tensions ran high among both Rebels and Yankees, especially in the war's latter stages, and with Union victory within reach by late 1864, it appeared that all bets were off as to what was or was not up for grabs. Though Sherman would later write in his memoirs that areas cleared of Confederate control were to be protected, the March 23, 1865 edition of the *Phoenix* reported a starkly contradictory account of Union men wasting little time exacting their revenge on that particular Rebel city:

The Burning of Columbia, South Carolina, February 17, 1865 by William Waud. From *Harper's Weekly*, April 8, 1865. *Library of Congress.*

> *Hardly had the troops reached the head of Main street, when the work of pillage was begun. Stores were broken open in the presence of thousands within the first hour after their arrival. The contents, when too cumbrous for the plunderers, were cast into the streets. Gold and silver, jewels and liquors, were eagerly sought...The officers [and] soldiers all seemed to consider it a matter of course. And woe to him who carried a watch with gold chain pendant; or who wore a choice hat, or overcoat, or boots or shoes. He was stripped by ready experts in the twinkling of an eye.*[12]

Now, it is in no way a reasonable, responsible or maybe even sane argument to try to blame everything on the British or the North. Though it may seem an easy case to make, to be sure it is roundly inaccurate, unfair and, if nothing else, just plain lazy to generalize the fate of Charleston's missing heirlooms. Indeed, there are examples of enemy compassion in the Lowcountry. Recollecting the disposition of a Rebel surgeon's corpse, which had fallen into Yankee hands after the Battle of Port Royal, Mary Whilden of Charleston poignantly wrote:

His remains were cared for by the Federal officers, one of whom having a mingling of Southern blood in his veins, was touched by the noble appearance of the fallen officer, and before interring his remains, took from his pockets his watch, case of instruments and whatever of value he had upon his person, then cut a lock of his hair and placed them with his handkerchief, upon which was marked his name, in a place of safety.[13]

Eventually, the deceased surgeon's brother arrived to claim the body, whereupon the Yankee commander immediately "turned over…the mementoes he had saved with the hope at some future day of restoring them to the family of the deceased."[14]

Of further note are the even rarer instances of lowly privates actually listening to their consciences. When Emma Judd of Connecticut received a silk bookmark from a Northern soldier with whom she was acquainted, his enclosed letter noted that although he had wanted to send her a memento and removed the bookmark "out of a family bible in one of the beautiful Southern houses," he still acted with considerable restraint. His comrades conversely were "helping themselves to anything and everything they wanted."[15]

Silk bookmark with pierced paper decoration taken from "one of the beautiful Southern houses" and sent north circa 1865. *Private collection; photo by Sean Money*.

More than Whilden's and Judd's recollections, however, one has to take into consideration simple geography and its role in both conflicts. American Patriots did not take the war overseas and physically invade England; thus there were no opportunities for them to carry out unrighteous looting on enemy home turf. Would they have if given that opportunity? If the manner in which Carolina Loyalists were treated after the war is any indication, most historians are quick to answer with a resounding "yes."

Likewise, it is vital to note that the Civil War was fought primarily in Confederate territory and the sharply divided border states of Missouri and Kentucky. There were only a few serious attempts by Confederate forces to invade Northern territory—the Maryland Campaigns in 1862, Pennsylvania in 1863 and the events of General Jubal Early's Valley Campaigns in 1864—thus offering only limited opportunities to harass, raid or exact punishment on Northern homesteaders. Unfortunately, this lopsidedness makes it difficult to even venture a guess as to what might have happened had the war been fought equally in the North and the South.

Of those few Confederate incursions into Northern regions, though, whatever Southern soldiers might or might not have been doing to private citizens there was of no concern to Charlestonians, most tending—and perhaps preferring—to view those events as eye-for-an-eye-type situations. Homesteaders in Virginia, Tennessee, Georgia, South Carolina and elsewhere had suffered greatly at the hands of the Union by 1864. In Charleston, Yankee batteries on Morris Island had been purposefully targeting civilians, intermittently lobbing shells and incendiaries into the city since the previous August. Therefore, in the eyes of the locals, whatever misery could be inflicted upon Yankee civilians on their turf indeed should be—and with as much force and ruthlessness as possible.

Attitudes of vengeance among Charlestonians became even more evident by mid-1864. In July, for example, vowing to give the Northern public "a taste of the horrors of war," General Early ordered troops to enter Chambersburg, Pennsylvania, and held the town ransom before systematically destroying it. His men broke into homes, smashed whatever furniture found therein and used the splintered fragments as kindling for house fires. Early himself later opined, "The value of the houses destroyed…with their contents, was fully $100,000 in gold."[16]

Yet even in the days prior to Chambersburg's fiery fate, the *Charleston Mercury* newspaper had already ardently defended Early's plans for revenge as being not just morally justified but perhaps not harsh enough. Printing one of many reports of the varied Southern exploits into what was then foreign soil on July 27, 1864:

Let this comfort the tens of thousands of houseless Confederates whose homes have been destroyed by Yankee raiders…It is impossible to be very angry with our soldiers; impossible to help admiring and loving the placable [sic] gentleness of theirs, which is so bright a contrast to the coarse brutality of those barbarians whom the Yankees have gathered up from the black slums of creation to pour over our field…To Confederate Troops the duty of retaliation is hard and odious; to retaliate everything in kind, indeed, would be altogether impossible for them…If our people are to be treated as rebels against their enemies, and thus visited with military execution by fire and sword—and if we either cannot or will not, when we have it in our power, pay slaughter with slaughter, pillage with pillage, conflagration with conflagration, then we fear that our doom is sealed.

Of course, Charlestonians by this time were already well versed in what damage enemy soldiers were capable of inflicting—and not just those wearing blue uniforms. Most locals then suffering through the "War of Northern Aggression" were themselves not far removed from the last century's humiliations meted out to their parents and grandparents by the redcoats. Even then, there was an overwhelming sense of loss throughout the city, and a mere eight decades was nowhere near long enough to ease the pain of those past victimizations.

Plundering was no less permitted among the British. They, too, had in place a series of laws dating back to 1765 (similar in most respects to the 1806 U.S. stipulations) that strictly prohibited "abuses or disorders which may be committed by any Officer or Soldier," including beating, rioting and extortion, among others. While these rules might have looked good on paper, though, they simply could not hold up in real-time war situations. Still, there were efforts by British officers to curb looting. For example, Admiral Mariot Arbuthnot, who in 1780 issued dire warnings to his sailors to keep off South Carolina coastal properties and threatened severe punishment to those who did not, occasionally prosecuted looters. So did the British army. Such were the cases of the Forty-seventh Regiment's Jonathon Marquin and James Donaldson, who, upon the conclusion of their May 26, 1780 court-martial in Charleston, were sentenced to a whopping "500 lashes" each for "attempting to rob the House of an Inhabitant."[17]

While not unique, judgments such as these were certainly uncommon in Charleston. By the time the city itself was under siege, varied attacks on noncombatant Patriots beyond the peninsula were regular occurrences—and usually violent ones to boot. Residents there incurred much damage to

Hessians on the March, circa 1780. *Courtesy of the Charleston Museum.*

both their homes and psyches. Thus, with two-hundred-plus battles and skirmishes taking place in South Carolina during the Revolution, there is no shortage of lurid tales involving British soldiers or their Hessian counterparts wantonly destroying loads of furniture and personal effects, not to mention the houses that held them.

The presence of Hessian units only added to the local turmoil. Widespread propaganda of the time depicted these men, feared all over the state, as killers, arsonists, Old World barbarians and even cannibals—with a taste for children, no less. While their supposed reputations were a bit exaggerated, Hessian troops, like their British cohorts, helped themselves to any number of household spoils, including slaves. Hessian infantry commander Johann von Ewald wrote of his own unit's abuses on civilians and their Lowcountry

Amy Legare's Chinese porcelain pitcher recovered from a Hessian camp near Calhoun Street, circa 1780. *Courtesy of the Charleston Museum.*

properties, but he was also quick to note the unquenchable hatred jeered at them by "the country people." "They hated us," he wrote from James Island, "from the bottom of their hearts."[18]

Amy Legare Baker was one of them. Having married Charleston merchant John Baker in 1767 and moved out to her husband's plantation, barely eleven years had passed before Amy found herself desperately getting herself, her children and their belongings back into Charleston in advance of enemy forces. After the capitulation, several Hessian soldiers made their way into the Bakers' dwelling. Not understanding Amy's protests in English—and perhaps not caring either—the soldiers casually pilfered several items, not the least of which was an elegant Chinese porcelain pitcher that dated to about 1720. A day later, still incensed at the Hessians' brashness, Amy marched resolutely to their encampment, near present-day Calhoun Street, to demand the return of her property. Amazingly, she somehow convinced a commanding officer to allow her access into the barracks, whereupon "the lost pitcher was recovered, and found to be full of fresh butter."[19]

Sadly, occupying British troops continued their countless depredations at the expense of the citizens and their belongings, even after news of the 1781 defeat at Yorktown reached Charleston. Finally, by December 13, 1782, over a year since Cornwallis's surrender in Virginia, British troops began evacuating the city—but not before helping themselves to several thousand slaves, the bells of St. Michael's Church and hundreds of rice barrels filled with estate and ecclesiastical silver, ceramics, jewelry, books and untold numbers of other miscellaneous prizes. Estimates taken soon after the war ended surmised that silver alone accounted for nearly £300,000 of the looted goods, a small portion of which redcoats had brazenly taken from Lemprière's Point barely twenty-four hours before their last ship left.[20]

Obviously, whatever material losses Charleston families suffered through the course of the war paled in comparison to the trauma of bloody warfare. For many wives and children, personal belongings likely meant little when compared to the death of a husband or father. Still, this immeasurable loss of goods and valuables significantly and seriously compounded the overall effects of the war on its citizenry.

II

A (ONCE) GOOD LIFE

It is noteworthy—and shameful—that Charleston's colonial legacy as a rich and influential city had been practically wiped from the public's memory by the twentieth century. Making this loss even more regrettable, by the mid-1700s, the southern colonies controlled upward of half the wealth in Britain's mainland empire, and Charleston sat convincingly at the pinnacle of this economic powerhouse. More remarkably still, Lowcountry planters and merchants were on average four to a staggering ten times richer than their northern counterparts.[21]

Indubitably, published material recounting Charleston's neglected—nigh forgotten—historic grandeur is relatively easy to find, but its basic economic history, for the most part, remains in the back pages of academic publications and amazingly still comes as a surprise to city visitors. As late as 1985, one specific examination of British North American colonial markets finds author John J. MacCusker noting that "Rice and Indigo have received less attention than tobacco; Charleston has attracted less interest than Philadelphia or Boston; and the demography of the Lower South has been neglected by comparison with the Chesapeake tidewater or the New England town." There are myriad reasons why proper recognition or even basic knowledge of Charleston's ascendancy and economic prowess waned after the Civil War, some of it as simple as the actual financial decline in the postwar years. As contemporary business faded, so too did the memories of its prominent planters, merchants and artisans who had propelled the earlier economy, until even their ghosts vanished in the decades between Reconstruction and the early twentieth century. As one Massachusetts art collector and author wrote, and probably believed, the South had less elegance because New England "was the richest in craftsmen." Well, was it? Hardly.[22]

The city's opponents—be they social, economic, political or military—knew the city to be the nucleus of southern wealth. Yet with plenty of documentation describing upper-crust Charlestonians rolling in cash and consequently surrounded with high-end finery, it still begs the question: how come so many still fail to realize this? As any antique-savvy person knows nowadays, Charleston pieces sold at auction or among private dealers can and do bring in record sums, an upward momentum that continuously brings to light a local artifact's survival through the centuries, all the while spreading greater awareness of southern decorative arts. Thus, local artisans and their masterpieces, when linked together with the immense estates of the city's elite, reveal a progressive and cosmopolitan culture that, until very recently, remained a grossly under-celebrated feature of southern teaching and equally underrepresented in literature and galleries outside the former Confederate states. So, in short, what took so long?

Alas, it is a simple answer. Returning to his Charleston home after the Revolutionary War, General William Moultrie noted with great sadness what his British adversaries had left in their wake:

> *It was the most dull, melancholy, dreary ride that any one could possibly take,* [the lands and properties] *had been so completely chequered by the different parties that no one part of it had been left unexplored; no living creature was to be seen except now and then a few scavengers (viz. buzzards), picking the bones of some unfortunate fellows who had been shot or cut down and left in the woods above ground…My plantation I found to be a desolate place; stock of every kind taken off; the furniture carried away.*[23]

Whatever the far-reaching effects of enemy theft on Charleston after each war, they are, and likely always will be, impossible to enumerate. Only spotty estimates and assumptions survive from the 1780s and 1860s. Add to this the natural disasters and conflagrations occurring throughout Charleston's history, and it is really no surprise that earlier twentieth-century visitors and tourists to the "Holy City" left it with the skewed perception of a hollowed-out remnant of a former great metropolis.

Even the A-list scholars forgot. It was Joseph Downs, the distinguished curator of the Metropolitan Museum's American Wing, who, during the 1949

Williamsburg Antiques Forum, made a rather colossal blunder in stating that "little of artistic merit was made south of Baltimore." For Downs, it was an honest mistake, but one that only helped to solidify the lingering malaise and humdrum attitude surrounding Charleston at the time. Thankfully, Downs's ridiculous declaration did not sit well with the southerners in attendance, with one unhesitant woman calling him out and openly asking him whether his words were of "prejudice or ignorance."[24]

The truth is, even in the first days of its 1670 founding, Charleston's mission was to make money. Anthony Ashley Cooper, First Earl of Shaftesbury, visualized an unparalleled British settlement, a "great port town" situated between two waterways that were "so convenient for public Commerce that it rather seems to be the design of some skillful Artist than the accidental position of nature." Though Cooper died in 1683, the rest of the world would not have to wait long for his lofty aspirations to reach near-complete fruition.[25]

Early settlers capitalized on as many Lowcountry natural resources as possible, all the while thoroughly studying which cash crops might flourish in the Carolina climate. Casual endeavors in silk, flax and oranges were moderately successful, but most of Charleston's early exports were naval stores (tar, pitch, turpentine) and timber "fit for masts…both pine and cypress." The deerskin trade with Native American tribes became quite lucrative and greatly supplemented England's demand for leather. In the eighteenth century, however, various agricultural commodities took hold, including the biggest moneymaker Charlestonians could have ever hoped for: *Oryza sativa*, better known as rice.[26]

It is not completely certain just how rice initially came to the South Carolina Lowcountry. Some sources claim one of the first settlers in the colony, Dr. Henry Woodword, either brought with him or was given a bag of rice from Madagascar, while others report that the first seeds were in the possession of imported Africans from possibly Senegal or Gambia. No matter the source, rice soon filled up Carolina's southeastern tidelands—and its planter's pocketbooks—as the most lucrative export. A total of 44,081 tons of rice left the port of Charleston in the 1720s, with nearly 100,000 tons being shipped the following decade. By 1761, a single barrel of "Carolina Gold" was valued at forty shillings, and by 1770, that price ballooned to three pounds, ten shillings. Rice led a long list of lucrative exports, and the wealth generated from these products, in turn, brought a vast array of imports to satisfy the wants and needs of the planter-merchant elites. In conclusion, this trade activity made Charleston and its port the economic engine of the southern colonies.[27]

Tragically, of course, the triumph that was rice came entirely on the backs of imported slaves. Many of those brought from Africa already had a comprehensive understanding of the complexities of growing and harvesting it. Though their Charleston masters would enjoy a new era of prosperity, it was a remarkably different story for those suffering enslavement. Nevertheless, their numbers and rice-growing knowhow were "a considerable Part of the Riches of the Province," and by the early 1700s, their value as property was an essential component in Charleston's money machine.[28]

Because of their value, in fact, it was occasionally slaves themselves who ended up as spoils of war. For example, in 1779, besides having his home robbed of numerous valuables, Henry Middleton lost eighty slaves from properties on the Combahee River when British detachments forcibly removed them. After the substantial loss, Henry spent his remaining years petitioning for reparations. If nothing else, perhaps the sheer cost of slaves helps to explain why Middleton fought so hard to reclaim his. For those who bought them, slaves were a serious investment. In the years before South Carolina secession, for example, plantation owners were paying upward of $1,200 each for "prime field hands," which adjusts to about $33,000 in 2013 currency. Nathaniel Heyward provides perhaps the greatest example of the conspicuous capital invested in human chattel. When the "richest man in South Carolina" died in 1851, his estate—a virtual kingdom—consisted of over forty-five thousand acres of rice fields and 2,334 slaves spread out over nineteen separate properties. With the addition of his Charleston residences, Heyward's cumulative holdings were appraised at the staggering sum of $2,018,000, nearly half of which was in slaves. It stands to reason, then, that many Charleston planters were nearly bankrupted upon having their slaves taken by enemy armies. Not only had much money gone into their purchase, but their sudden absence as a field labor force brought plantation production and ensuing income to a dead stop.[29]

It is no wonder, then, why even Charleston Loyalists felt looted by their British protectors after Sir Henry Clinton put forth his Philipsburg Proclamation in 1779. This document pledged freedom and security to those in bondage who abandoned their masters for British camps. Though Clinton's intention was to deprive the Patriots of their labor force, thousands of slaves belonging to Loyalist families escaped as well, costing those estates thousands in lost production and property. Making matters worse, redcoats and Hessians thought nothing of forcing these escaped men, women and children back to work digging fortifications, driving livestock and hauling artillery. Thus, after discovering that the British army's forced labor was even

A List of Negroes belonging to Henry Middleton which were taken from his several Plantations on Combahee River in the Year 1779, carried to Georgia & East Florida chiefly by McGirt & his Party.

Upper Place

Harry McDonal
Silvia — Dead. SP
Cato — Cornick
L. Harry — Dunford
Quash
Kate
Bob
Bella
Limus
Beck — McMoon
Nelly
Mary & Child — Indians
Ned & Child — d
Phillis & Child
Doctor — McYork
Stephen — Dead
Phillis — Dead. CW
Pompey — Woods
Affey & Child L.
Dick — McTeora
Sawny & Child — home
Sarry — Dead
L. WM — Indians
Paul
Achrum

Middle Place

Galins — McJohn
Rachael
Affey
Lolly
Elvey
Warkey — McHopkins
G. Cato — Anderson
Gitta — Dead
Fina
Formarry
L. Tom — Indians
Cyrus
Hercules — Indians
James
Comboy
George
Frank
Sy
Quash
Hercules
Pompey
Tom
Titus
Will
Bush
Cuffy
Adam
Balaam
Ben
Liscinda
Venus
Jeffery

Lower Place

Charles
Joe
Hester
Cathy
Seth
Beck
Venus
Tom
Answer
Caesar
Cupid.

From the New Sett:

Scipio
Hector
Peter
Bob
Will
March
Robin
Coleman

From Ponpon

Primas.

Partial list of Middleton slaves confiscated from their Combahee River rice plantations. *Courtesy of Middleton Place Foundation.*

worse than the plantation life from which they had fled, many slaves escaped and went back to their original masters.[30]

As for more leisurely times of peace—the awfulness of slavery notwithstanding—Charleston elites relished the fruits of their rich endeavors. They traveled, they collected, they entertained and they spent. They were well versed in science, literature and socialization, sparing no expense when accumulating works for their private libraries or sponsoring various entertainments.

> *All the new publications in London, and many of the most valuable books, both ancient and modern, have been imported for the use of this society; the members of which* [are] *ambitious of proving themselves the worthy descendants of British Ancestors…For amusement, the inhabitants of Charlestown had not only books and public papers, but also assemblies, balls, concerts, and plays, which were attended by companies almost equally brilliant as those of any town in Europe of the same size.*[31]

Moreover, no one of means skimped in building his urban estate. The elite commissioned the latest architectural styles and embellished every room with fashionable, albeit massively expensive, silver, ceramics, furniture and fine art, both imported and domestically made. "It was natural for [Charlestonians] to take pride in the possession of…finished workmanship and beautiful design," reflected a local newspaper." A background of gracious living demanded it."[32]

Besides the planters, Charleston merchants and artisans provided an essential backbone for the city's thriving economy—so much so that it was not at all odd for them, through their talent and success, to attain the same wealth, status and reputation as the landed elite. Men like these far outnumbered the planters, and through their trade prowess, they amassed veritable stockpiles of saleable goods capable of fulfilling almost any desire. Dozens of Charleston families with instantly recognizable names—Manigault, Laurens, Wragg, Huger—all rose to the same level as the planter class through their merchant, trade or artisan origins.[33]

Of course, the negative side to all this was that Charleston's widespread success and wealth unwittingly made it an attractive, desirable mark. Symbolism aside, city wealth served to enhance its appeal to the enemy. "If we cannot destroy the…resources of the Province," wrote Henry Clinton in 1779, "we shall accomplish nothing substantial for Great Britain." For sure, then, during the time of the redcoat and Yankee occupations, loot-minded soldiers could choose just about any Charleston house at random and probably find rich rewards within.[34]

Still, some homes just looked better than others, and one example, built by Charleston merchant Miles Brewton, still serves as a terrific reminder of such. The grandson of a silversmith, Brewton greatly expanded his inherited and marital wealth by making sizeable fortunes through the sale of dry goods, land and slaves. His success, in fact, remains clearly visible in his 1769 home—a dominant Palladian-styled, double-pile house that took four years and £8,000 sterling to complete. However, its commanding presence also helps to explain why enemy generals chose it not once but twice as their headquarters. Sir Henry Clinton resided there first in 1780, despite the presence of Brewton's widowed sister, Rebecca Motte, and her three daughters, all of whom the mother kept partially secluded while she catered to the needs of the general and his staff. In 1865, Union brigadier general Alexander Schimmelfennig commandeered the house as headquarters for the 127th New York Volunteers and the 21st U.S. Colored Troops and from which his soldiers launched so-called tours of liberation that "went everywhere breaking into homes and helping themselves to whatever they wanted, cursing and raving at the inhabitants all the while."[35]

Interestingly, tangible evidence of the occupiers' contempt for Brewton's house remains, and its existence has become a noteworthy tidbit in Charleston's rich history of war. One particular example, carved into an elegant marble undermantel, survives: British graffito depicting a relief caricature of Henry Clinton and various other signatures and scribblings.

Now, although it may be easy to examine the city's accomplished history by determining what it had, taking a close look at what it lost is most certainly a trickier exercise. Anyone endeavoring to look into Charleston's lost heirlooms and treasures even now will, unfortunately, albeit understandably, need to wade through numerous pages of angry, vengeful recollections. Indeed, Mark Twain may have been correct when he wrote that the ink of all written history is "merely fluid prejudice."[36]

In his journal, Methodist Episcopal bishop Francis Asbury found his 1794 visit to Charleston abhorrent due to the riches and excesses of its residents, noting, "I have had a time of deep dejection of spirits...loss of sleep, and trouble of soul...I now leave Charleston, the seat of Satan." Thus, it becomes painfully clear that Charleston was never without its share of detractors—nor was the citizenry itself ever fearful of making them. Problems with Great Britain after 1765 provoked a variety of different reactions among South Carolinians. Some believed their disputes could

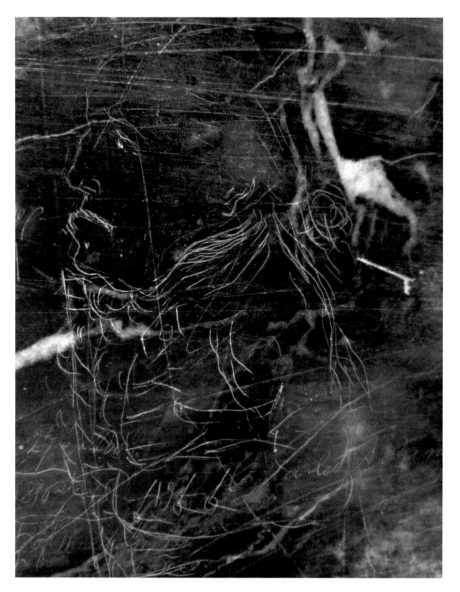

Crude relief of General Sir Henry Clinton scratched into a marble mantelpiece at the Miles Brewton House circa 1780. *Courtesy of Lee Manigault.*

be resolved peaceably, with others convinced that war was inevitable. Afterward, the nullification crises of the 1820s and '30s, followed by talk of secession throughout the 1850s, set Charleston apart—and not in a good way. By then, there was an undeniably obvious discord between the South and North, with many outsiders seeing Charleston, the "Holy City," place more unholy, stubborn and shameless than anywhere else.[37]

Thus, it is easy to become distracted when considering all the aggressively opinionated hullabaloo of period newspapers and the unrestricted, resentful writings of those victimized. One can most certainly call accuracy into question. Even eyewitness accounts can be a bit muddled, the writer's hatred in many cases clouding exact memory. The so-called Myers letter might be the best example of this dubiousness. Not only has it somehow withstood the test of time, but it regrettably still surfaces occasionally in postwar accounts of Carolina's Confederate history. On January 19, 1867, the *Charleston Daily News* reprinted a story from Columbia's *Daily Phoenix* that introduced a letter "found in the streets of Columbia immediately after the army of General Sherman left." Written by one Lieutenant Thomas J. Myers to his wife in Boston and dated February 26, 1865, the 643-word letter provided still shellshocked Carolinians with some of the most damning testimony as to exactly where their most valued possessions might have disappeared. Following are extracts from the letter as they appeared in each paper:

Camp near Camden, S.C. Feb. 26, 1865

My dear wife—I have no time for particulars. We have had a glorious time in this State. Unrestricted license to burn and plunder was the order of the day. The chivalry (meaning the Honourable & Chivalrous people of the South) have been stripped of most of their valuables. Gold watches, silver pitchers, cups, spoons, forks, &c., are as common in camp as blackberries. I have at least a quart of jewelry for you and all the girls, and some No. 1 diamond rings and pins among them. General Sherman has silver and gold enough to start a bank...All the general officers and many besides had valuables of every description, down to embroidered ladies' pocket handkerchiefs. I have my share of them, too. We took gold and silver enough from the damned rebels to have redeemed their infernal currency twice over. Tell Sallie I am saving a pearl bracelet and ear-rings for her; these were taken from the Misses Jamison, daughters of the President of the South Carolina Secession Convention.[38]

Of course, even if this document did originate in Camden and somehow managed to migrate to Columbia only to be left drifting in the streets as the newspaper suggests, there was only one lieutenant in the entire Federal army named Thomas Myers, an unwed midwesterner in the Seventeenth Indiana

Infantry. Worse, Myers was positioned somewhere between the Alabama border and Nashville, nowhere near Sherman or South Carolina, at the time the letter was composed. It makes sense then that the Myers letter is a likely forgery, written and planted perhaps by some vindictive soul looking to keep the state's collective anger alive in 1867.[39]

Fortunately, at least when it comes to actual missing artifacts, heirlooms and materials, no matter the bias, bitterness, bereavement or betrayal directed at wayward Yankee or redcoat marauders, the object in question was physically taken; was it not? If the item were here before the enemy arrived and gone after he left, one does not require a super-powered sleuth squad to determine plundering as its cause for disappearance. Therefore, this pilfering of real artifacts is significantly easier to dissect than the hurtfulness surrounding its departure. Just as Shakespeare penned, "When Envy breeds unkind division: There comes the ruin." Class, culture, custom and capital saturated Charleston; its wealth made at least some of the opinions and motives of its green-eyed adversaries a bit easier to understand. Indeed, the city's conquest was a paramount objective and an outright grand prize for militaries on the outside looking in during the 1770s and '80s and again in the 1860s. For them, Charleston was a different kind of target—an aloof and pampered one—that, if not an eager participant in the rebellion of the eighteenth century, was the outright seed of it in the nineteenth. If this symbolism alone were not reason enough for sacking, the city's incredible wealth most assuredly was.[40]

III

DEFILERS AT THE DOOR

Writing from Yonge's Island, Eliza Wilkinson voiced her extreme disappointment at the "gentlemanly" British forces heading for Charleston in 1779:

> *You know we had always heard most terrible accounts of the actions of the British troops at the northward; but, (fool that I was,) I thought they must be exaggerated, for I could not believe that a nation so framed for humanity, and many other virtues, should come in so short a time, divest themselves of even the least trace of what they once were...Yet, sometimes, when I heard fresh accounts of their cruelty to our northern brethren when in their power, I cannot repress my indignation against the barbarous, hard-hearted Briton's, (how changed their character!) At length I heard they had got possession of the Georgia State, and used the inhabitants cruelly, paying no respect to age or sex...Thousands would I have given to have been in any part of the globe where I might not see them, or to have been secure from their impending evils, which were ready to burst over our heads.* [41]

Eventually, Eliza found out firsthand just what the enemy was capable of. Though she hoped in subsequent letters to be spared the ugliness of redcoat looting, it was not to be. Inevitably, they showed up. Soldiers sacked the main house, smashed open trunks and overturned furniture while troops remaining outside held some of the women at gunpoint, forcing them to hand over whatever jewelry they had on them and even stealing the silver shoe buckles right off Eliza's and her sister's feet.[12]

Eliza Wilkinson's ordeal was by no means singular. Widespread reports of wayward redcoat marauders along the Lowcountry tidelands consistently stirred the anxieties of plantation dwellers, and those stuck in the enemy's path soon came to understand their own peril. Most made for especially easy targets. According to a frustrated letter from Richard Lorentz of James Island to whatever British officer might read it, not even solitary widows were spared. Writing on behalf of a "Mrs. Keir," Lorentz stated that despite the woman having "no Relations at all in arms against [the] Government" and that she "never had anything to do with the present disturbances," she "has been once already stripped by a party of soldiers, and is very much afraid she will lose all she has got."[13]

In truth, British forces by this time had a major score to settle with Charleston, having been wholly humiliated at the Battle of Fort Sullivan three years earlier on June 28, 1776. After all, it was on that astonishing day that 435 rough militiamen—within an unfinished wooden fortification, no less—fought off nine of Commodore Peter Parker's heavily armed British warships, damaging four of them and killing more than 100 Brits. The fallout from this startling American victory was felt throughout London and turned George III's throne into quite the hot seat seemingly overnight. The *London Chronicle* in particular was relentless in its send-ups of the Crown and Parker, jovially regaling its readers with the unfortunate injury he suffered upon having his breeches blown off by a Patriot cannonball. Thus, when the redcoats came back to Charleston a few years later, they were more than eager to exact their long overdue punishment on "one of the obstinate daughters of America."[14]

It was not long before Patriots—and even some Loyalists—understood that something in this army had changed. Truly, as exemplified by their actions against people like Keir, this was an army of an altogether different lot—they were angrier, tougher, resentful and, moreover, frustrated by a war they thought should have been won already. Commanding officers, feeling immense pressure from London to rein in the southern states, imparted a clear message: losing the region a second time would cost the empire dearly and most assuredly provide hard evidence of royal decline. As for the soldiers themselves, theirs was a more frustrated motive. Consistent letters from families back home effectively reminded each that, as the war expanded, so did its cost for their loved ones. Tax increases were hitting every Briton hard. Trade and mercantilism were off. Employment was dwindling. In London, Whitehall was tearing itself apart over how best

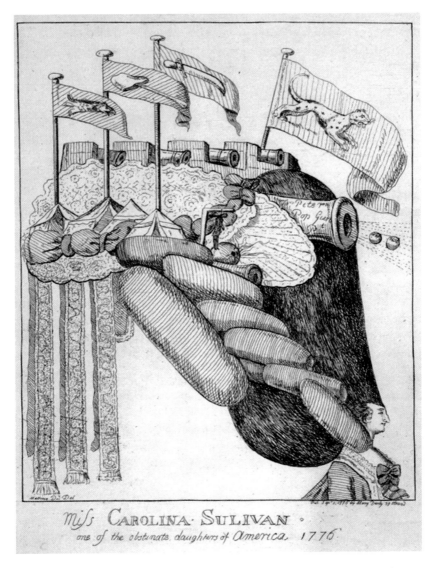

Miss Carolina Sulivan [sic]—*One of the Obstinate Daughters of America* by Matthew Darly, circa 1776, published in London ridiculing the British loss at Sullivan's Island. *Library of Congress.*

to manage the war and stabilize the economy, prompting one newspaper to rename several of the "justices" within the government as "Just-Asses." Meanwhile, another political cartoon illustrated the severed heads of several prominent government officials impaled atop pikes at the town gates, the caption suggesting the "Heads of a nation in a right situation."[15]

Whether or not the regularly bad news from back east motivated or deflated the average British fighter was irrelevant. Which was worse anyhow—a vengeful soldier or an anxious one? Either way, by the spring and summer of 1780, Charlestonians would see the redcoats for what the war with America had made them. Like Eliza Wilkinson, residents recollected how the soldiery had morphed into a more brutal enemy, one describing them as "a new set, greatly inferior in education and good breeding…From an army abounding with such unworthy characters, and stationed among a people whom they hated as rebels…it was not reasonable to expect that winning behavior which was necessary to conciliate the affections of the revolted States."[46]

For specific examples of such savagery, one need look no further than the gruesome fieldwork of Sir Banastre "Bloody" Tarleton, who considered the terrorization of civilians a "point of duty" and, by 1780, had come to embody the tattered virtues of British forces in the southern states. Charlestonians, to be sure, were quite familiar with his brutalities both on and off the battlefield, even in the days before the city's capitulation. Even General Francis Marion took note, stating in a letter to Horatio Gates that Tarleton and his men had "burnt all of the houses and destroyed all the corn" along an approximately sixty-mile stretch between Camden and Nelson's Ferry. Far worse, three of his troops raped at least three women sheltering at a plantation belonging to John Colleton, a staunch Loyalist.[47]

Of course, even if Tarleton had never set foot in Carolina, there were still plenty of enemy raiders around to keep the locals' blood boiling. "The life of no man was safe," wrote one local fellow. "The country was full of rascally 'bush-whackers.'" Thus, as Tarleton, Clinton and their ilk plowed through the region, Patriot-supporting civilians soon faced an obvious, albeit difficult and painful, decision: run for cover or stay put and pray. Indeed, many women and children did flee the countryside, withdrawing to Charleston and leaving their homes and plantations wide open to enemy predation. Only at war's end would these families wholly discover what innumerable ancestral treasures had been lost, stolen or destroyed.[48]

The pain of lost valuables did not begin or end in Patriot homes only. American victory subsequently branded plenty of remaining Loyalists as *personae non gratae* in their own homeland. As one officer put it: "The poor, unhappy loyalists who the British government…had most solemnly pledged its faith to protect…were now to be left victims of their merciless enemies." Fortunately, many of these homesteaders read the proverbial handwriting on the wall and in 1782 simply packed up and sailed back to England, some leaving with the troops themselves. Others left for Canada, Florida or the

West Indies. As for those who could not—or would not—abandon their lands, however, the tables were turned on them almost immediately.[49]

The state of South Carolina went on a warpath all its own after independence was won, holding those who sided with the British accountable and flat-out punishing those who helped them. Charleston Loyalists—"subjects of his Britannic Majesty," as the General Assembly preferred to call them—quickly faced their own version of enemy looters, this time in the form of state lawmakers free from any royal oversight. The lucky ones lost only their money, the state taxing or otherwise amercing them to the point of homelessness. Other Loyalists like Paul Hamilton, unfortunately, had far heavier reparations to make.[50]

Inheriting acreages on both Edisto and James Islands, Hamilton had prospered before the war with Britain and made it clear from the beginning that he would not support any move toward American independence. He eventually sailed off to Bermuda and later the Bahamas rather than face life as a Loyalist neck-deep in a pro-Patriot region. To his neighbors, it was a cowardly tactic and for sure one that did not sit well with the rest of the rabblerousing public. In their minds, since Hamilton was born a native of Carolina and profited because of it, he should defend his homeland from the tyranny of the Britons.[51]

Eventually, money problems brought Hamilton back home, but his allegiance to the Crown remained steadfast. Hamilton had done as much as he could to help his British brethren, even allocating one of his slaves, Lymus, to guide the redcoats through James Island. As if that were not enough, he went on to sign a formal address to Sir Henry Clinton in 1780 declaring his allegiance—an affront that South Carolina Patriots would not soon forget.[52]

The Patriots' ultimate victory was an especially bitter defeat for Hamilton. On February 26, 1782, Governor John Rutledge, supported by the General Assembly, put forth an estate confiscation act essentially seizing any and all Loyalist properties. To be sure, it was a law born of revenge.

> *It is evident that it was the fixed determination of the enemy, notwithstanding their professions to the contrary, to treat this State as a conquered country; and that the inhabitants were to expect the utmost severities, and to hold their lives, liberties, and properties, solely at the will of His Britannic Majesty's officers; and it is therefore inconsistent with public justice and policy, to afford protection any longer to the property of British subjects.*
>
> *Be it therefore enacted...That all the real estates, either in possession, reversion, or remainder, of the several persons...known to be subjects of his Britannic Majesty...are hereby declared to be fully seized and possessed.*

Sherman's March to the Sea by Felix O.C. Darley, circa 1868. *Library of Congress.*

Be it further enacted by the authority aforesaid, that instead of inflicting capital punishment on such persons, they shall be, and they are hereby declared to be, forever banished from this State.[53]

Hamilton was doomed. Returning to England penniless, he tried for the next several years to recoup what he had lost, even going before a Loyalist clearing committee "for enquiring into the Losses and Services of the American Loyalists." Conservatively estimating his seized assets at around £10,000 sterling, he put forth a lengthy inventory of just what backing his fellow Brits had cost him, including a sardonic £900 "loss sustained by being plundered by British soldiers [of] General [Augustine] Prevost's Army."[54]

England never repaid Hamilton, and his ordeal became a cautionary tale relished among the newly independent Americans and lamented by the vanquished Loyalists. Even a poem was written about his woes after the war:

An humble loyalist, unknown to fame,
And Hamilton my name.
On the small wreck of a once plenteous store
I live, nor ever wish my little more,
Save when afflicted Virtue I perceive,
And want the means that Virtue to Relieve.[55]

In the roundly defeated state of Georgia, Sherman's dreadful—yet admittedly effective—"March to the Sea" ended on December 22, 1864, when he famously presented President Abraham Lincoln with the city of Savannah as an early Christmas gift. Although some modern historians living outside the Carolinas still tend to view this gesture as the endgame of Sherman's southern adventure, Charlestonians know better. Most South Carolinians of the era, in fact, needed but a newspaper to know that, for them, Sherman's march had only just begun, and the line between battle front and home front would soon blur.

Charleston citizens of the early 1860s had grown up hearing varied stories of British marauders from the previous century. What was more, each had a gut feeling that Union troops, if given the opportunity, would behave just as poorly and probably worse. "You'll regret the day you ever done it," wrote Joseph Harrison lamentably on his personal copy of the *Charleston Mercury Extra* announcing South Carolina's secession. For him and many others, their own common sense told them that Charleston—the place where the whole mess started in 1861—would be made to pay for

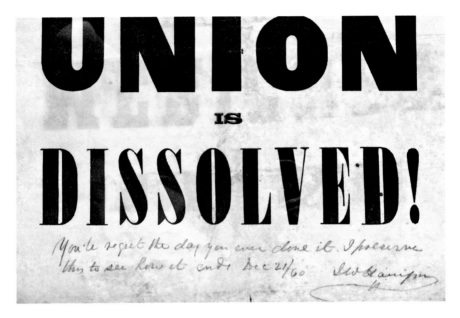

The December 20, 1860 *Charleston Mercury Extra* belonging to Joseph Harrison, who inscribed the following on the bottom: "You'll regret the day you ever done it. I preserve this to see how it ends." *Courtesy of the Charleston Museum.*

its sins against the Federal government should the South lose its fight for independence.[56]

Even long before secession, those with somewhat hesitant hearts—or perhaps cooler heads—warned of dire consequences should their move toward sovereignty fail. Urging South Carolinians to think twice about secession as early as 1835, Governor George McDuffie issued his personal warning:

> *You would be in unceasing alarm from the incursions of these friends whom your leaders have taken such pains to sour and irritate and convert into deadly enemies. It is well known that the hostility of friends converted into enemies, is always far more embittered, and attended with more of ferocious outrage than that of nations between which no ties of friendship have ever existed. Ponder well, fellow citizens, on these things…will you not look before you leap? Accursed—yea, ten-fold accursed, be the man, however gifted by nature or fortune, or standing in society, who dares to lay sacrilegious hands on the sacred ark of our safety, The Union of the States.*[57]

Despite this and other assorted pleas, however, most Charlestonians stayed the course with the Confederacy, never really minding the underlying dangers and uncertainties of taking on the United States and its military. "There will be a great struggle for Charleston," wrote Thomas Lynch to his brother. "But I do not believe they will ever be able to take it…I will believe it when I see it." Another Charleston resident, Mary Whilden, whose confidence in a quick and sure Southern victory vanished after the 1861 loss of Port Royal, was not as sure: "Up to this time, we felt our homes were not in danger, but this feeling of security did not linger long; the time soon came when it was thought best to send the women and children to places of safety. The days of refugeeing [sic] were about to begin, homes to be broken up, alas! how many forever."[58]

Of course, not helping to ease any domestic tensions were the local newspapers. Whatever their accuracy, by late 1863, Southern journalists were eloquently describing the latest atrocities at the hands of the Yankees while defiantly struggling to find good news for Charleston Confederates to rally around. Oftentimes, reporters, a bit too eager to boost morale, spun their stories significantly so as not to pile onto the public's uneasiness. Worse still, sometimes even good news turned out bad. On July 8, for example, a full five days after the fact, Charlestonians rejoiced upon reading the *Charleston Daily Courier*'s erroneous headline touting "General Lee's Victory" at the Battle of Gettysburg, a sentiment echoed by the *Charleston Mercury* as late as July 16. Alas, even more days passed before the city learned the staggering number of South Carolina casualties and the horrible truth of Confederate defeat. Thus, with reliability of battlefield accounts understandably shaky—and with many succeeding in scaring the living daylights out the readers—it was eventually left to the individual to decide whether the information was actually believable. As one frustrated Charlestonian wrote, "We hear of nothing but rumors of the war, one day contradicting what another had as fact, so much so, that I have lost all confidence in newspaper & telegraphic accounts."[59]

Despite wanting to take comfort from what the newspapers were telling them, letters sent home from soldiers at times told an altogether different story in far more factual terms. One such letter by Lieutenant Richard Lewis, an enlisted man in the Fourth Regiment South Carolina Volunteers, described to his mother just how horrid a home front war could be. From his encampment near Chattanooga on October 3, 1863, he wrote:

> *This is the hardest looking country I have ever served in yet, looking as if it had never been in a state of civilization. I suppose the reason of it is*

CHARLESTON.

WEDNESDAY MORNING, JULY 8, 1863.

General Lee's Victory.

The battle at Gettysburg disclosed the important fact that the whole of General LEE's army is in Pennsylvania. That event removed every doubt touching the nature of that movement. It was seen that it is not a raid, but a real campaign of vast proportions. The consummate General who, under God, holds in his hands the destinies of one hundred thousand men, comprising his command, had other and higher objects in view than the replenishment of his stores and the capture of fat cattle. He aimed to accomplish results which will be felt throughout the hostile land—results that will strike terror and dismay into the mean and boastful foe, and fill our own bosoms with gladness.

The July 8, 1863 *Charleston Courier* erroneously proclaiming General Robert E. Lee's "victory" at Gettysburg. *Courtesy of the* Post and Courier.

that the Yankees have been playing their same old game of destruction in our land, and what they have not laid waste to, our army have. Some of the poor women who ran off at the time of the last battle have come in and found their homes pillaged of everything, not even leaving them bedsteads standing, or a pound of meat or dust of meal or flour. So you see they are in a state of starvation, and their husbands being in the army cannot provide for them in any way, nor can they expect anything from the country after being sacked by Yankeedom. This is one of the bitter fruits of war.[60]

The summer of 1863 served as arguably the most terrible turning point of the war for Charleston. The capture of Vicksburg and the slaughter at Gettysburg were obvious topics of conversation, but far closer to home was the massive, pivotal and tragic siege of Morris Island and its eventual downfall. General Pierre Beauregard was well aware what a

Above: General View of Morris Island. From *Harper's Weekly*, August 22, 1863. *Courtesy of the Charleston Museum.*

Left: Empty grave of John C. Calhoun in St. Philip's graveyard. At the time of this 1865 photo, Calhoun's remains were still concealed on the other side of Church Street. *Library of Congress.*

Yankee-controlled Morris Island could mean for Charleston, and citing the previous, overzealous Union ransacking of Bluffton, South Carolina, he called enemy General Quincy Gillmore to task, urging him in an impassioned letter that he instruct his men to act mannerly should they gain access into the city. Indeed, Charlestonians were in a race against time. The city's livability was deteriorating and would get horribly worse by the end of the year. Thus, Charlestonians began to consider the reality of their enemies' sticky fingers, should they get in, and many started the rather panicked process of securing as many personal valuables as they could. One such individual, Robert Newman Gourdin, even went so far as to protect the deceased.[61]

Convinced that the remains of John C. Calhoun, member of the "Immortal Trio" and South Carolina's premier supporter of states' rights and nullification, would be far too tempting a prize for the Yankees, on the night of April 5, 1863, Gourdin began the somber work of exhuming, moving and hiding Calhoun's body in the St. Philip's Church graveyard. Gourdin morosely explained in a letter to Calhoun's son, Andrew, that with the help of several friends and sextons from both St. Philip's and neighboring French Huguenot Church, the work of protecting his father's mortal remains had begun in the late evening and continued well into the early morning. "We…succeeded in opening the tomb," he wrote. "The metallic coffin was transferred to a strong pine case and removed into the church." Unable to finish what they had started before daybreak, however, Gourdin and his crew suspended their mission until the following night, leaving Calhoun's body to spend the rest of that Monday stored discreetly and uprightly beneath a flight of stairs inside St. Philip's.[62]

Reconvening in near total darkness on April 6, Gourdin and his associates again went to work and quietly reburied Calhoun, this time in an unmarked grave on the eastern side of the churchyard, "east of the burial grounds of Captain James Welsman and immediately at the foot" of his family plot. "Should I survive this war," wrote Gourdin, "I will make it my duty to restore [Calhoun's remains] to their original place of deposit." Mercifully, Gourdin did fulfill his promise, but only after eight long years had passed.[63]

In the midst of the city's significantly destabilized state at the end of 1863, Charlestonians, like their Patriot forebears, again faced a heart-wrenching decision: whether to stay or go. However, unlike Benjamin Lincoln in 1780, who had essentially holed up both his army and Charleston's populace in an armadillo-styled defense on the peninsula, citizens bearing witness to the coming Yankee onslaught at least had some options as to where they might escape. Among the most appealing—and, at the time, most realistic—was flight to the state capital of Columbia.

Now, looking back at the dreadfulness that befell Columbia in the winter of 1865, when the city was plundered of nearly everything before being put to the torch, there arises a natural question: why there? Was fleeing to Columbia—the capital city of the very state that fired the first shots of the war, a place that surely fell immediately next in line to Charleston as a specific target for the Union—the wisest of destinations for evacuees carrying all of their families' worldly treasures?

William Gilmore Simms appears to have asked himself this same question shortly after war's end. While taking stock of Columbia's destruction, he recalled that much of the local reasoning followed the recommendation of authorities: "We assumed—and this idea was tacitly encouraged, if not believed, by the authorities, military and civil…that the bulk of [Sherman's] army was preparing for a descent upon Charleston."

Consequently, the obliteration of the Holy City, at least in the minds of its citizens and leaders, was a foregone conclusion. Writing to a "Dear Friend" in 1864, for instance, Charles Holst underscored this general feeling of doom: "Charleston will have a name in History beyond any other fight or city, but the Yankees will never give it up…it is the nest of the Rebellion and must be wiped from the Earth."[64]

Of course, what no Charlestonian could know by this point was that not even Sherman saw a need to kill a city—symbolic or not—that for all practical and strategic purposes was already dead. One needed only to take a quick look around at what remained of Charleston to ascertain that there was hardly anything left to conquer anyway. The way Sherman saw it, a lengthy federal siege—and an unrelated 1861 fire—had done his job for him, reducing the city to "a mere desolated wreck."[65]

To be sure, those who fled for Columbia with as many transportable possessions as possible would soon know it to be one of their more dreadful mistakes. But to be fair, it was not as if they had any real choice in staying put; they had to go somewhere. On August 22, 1863, immediately after General Gillmore's artillerists began lobbing shells into Charleston, Beauregard fired back with an angry letter explaining that he would begin the proper procedures to evacuate as many civilians as possible. Many believed that remaining in their Charleston homes was tantamount to death itself and headed out. "Matters were getting worse," noted Reverend Anthony Porter. "It was determined to hold Charleston to the last extremity, to fight street by street, if attacked, and orders were issued to remove all noncombatants from the City." Finally, with the city all but deserted on December 14, 1864, Major General Robert Ransom ordered: "On no account will non-combatants be allowed to enter the City of Charleston except in passing through to more interior portions of the State."[66]

Indeed, news of Sherman's movements through Georgia—and what was or was not on fire there—had served as consistent, albeit unwelcome, aide memoires of how incredibly dangerous lingering in Charleston might become. With each passing day as he and his men marched north from Savannah, more Charleston homesteaders moved north to Columbia. Some believed the rumors that large garrisons of entrenched Confederate soldiers were protecting the concentrated masses of coastal refugees. Still others went for no more reason than it was where everyone else was going. There was, after all, safety in numbers—or so they hoped. The more people in one place the better, right?

Columbia was naturally held to be one of the most secure places of refuge. It was never doubted that this city, which contained so many of the manufacturers of the Confederate Government, the Treasury, &c., would be defended with all the concentrated vigor of which the Confederacy was capable…numbers (of people) seemed to promise a degree of security not to be hoped for in any obscure rural abode.[67]

Unfortunately, that "concentrated vigor" that Columbia's Confederate defenders supposedly once had had long since evaporated. In truth, according to the *Columbia Phoenix*, "South Carolina is almost stripped of troops…Lacking volunteers, provisions, clothing, medicine, weapons, munitions of war, the country is exhausted, and farther struggle, under these circumstances must only involve the people at large—those who are incapable of arms—women and children, old men and boys—in a thousand miseries, the smallest form of which would be destitution."[68]

Maybe even more lamentable was the fact that with huge numbers of wealthy Charlestonians out of Charleston and in Columbia, that city was overcrowded with people and overstuffed with silver, gold, jewelry, fine art and plenty of other valued goods.

The city had accordingly doubled in population, and here also was to be found an accumulation of wealth, in [silver], jewels, pictures, books, manufactures of art and virtu, not to be estimated—not, perhaps, to be paralleled in any other town of the Confederacy. In many instances, the accumulations were those of a hundred years—of successive generations—in the hands of the oldest families of the South. A large proportion of the wealth of Charleston had been stored in the capital city…[69]

Columbia, then, more so than anywhere else, was ripe for the picking, and just about every Yankee soldier knew it. Even though General Ulysses S. Grant was nowhere near South Carolina while Sherman was traipsing through it, he still appeared cognizant of the massive stockpiles of plunder within the capital. Writing later in his memoirs, he noted, "Columbia…[was] regarded as so secure from invasion that the wealthy people of Charleston and Augusta had sent much of their valuable property…to be stored. Among the goods sent there were valuable carpets, tons of old Madeira, silverware, and furniture. I am afraid much of these goods fell into the hands of our troops."[70]

For a great many Charlestonians in 1865, their lost goods would be taken not from their empty homes on the peninsula but from their travel trunks, their pockets and, in some instances, their very hands. Noting in his journal how the state capital was "vastly more valuable to us in this campaign," Sherman's aide-de-camp, Major George Nichols, further observed, "It is the home of thousands of those wicked instigators to treason who have made this state so hated and despised...Columbia, therefore, is a richer prize...than any city in the South."[71]

IV

(Im)Proper Burials

"Somehow our men had got the idea that South Carolina was the cause of all our troubles," wrote Sherman in his memoirs. "Therefore on them should fall the scourge of war in its worst form…We would no longer be able to restrain our men as we had done in Georgia." By the end of February 1865, Charleston, unlike the capital, had managed to avoid the enemy's torch but not his sticky fingers. Almost immediately after the city's formal surrender, Yankee soldiers began storming off the beaches and boats and into the grandest houses they could find.[72]

As mayor of Confederate Charleston, Charles Macbeth had done all he could to manage his city in the face of defeat. Finally, on February 18, 1865, he ran out of options. Meeting with Lieutenant Colonel A.G. Bennett of the Twenty-first U.S. Colored Troops, Macbeth carried out his final act as an elected official by formally handing Charleston over to the Federal army.

Charles's wife, Henrietta Ravenel Macbeth, meanwhile, was understandably frightened. No doubt concerned for the safety of her husband, she was equally distraught over the family's heralded plantation home and the generations-old valuables therein. Built on a one-thousand-acre, 1688 land grant from the lords proprietors themselves, Henrietta's Ravenel forebears had named their plantation "Wantoot" after a nearby Native American settlement, and it had remained in her family ever since. By 1865, in fact, it was one of the oldest plantations in the Carolinas, and although the house and its holdings had escaped total destruction once

Marching On! From *Harper's Weekly*, March 18, 1865. The Fifty-fifth Massachusetts Colored Regiment entered Charleston on February 21, 1865. *Courtesy of the Charleston Museum.*

before in 1781, after being taken over by British colonel Alexander Stewart, Henrietta was not about to tempt fate again. Thus, leaving Charles behind in the city, she rushed to Berkeley County to see what, if anything, could be done before enemy troops arrived there.[73]

Henrietta scurried through Wantoot, doing her best to salvage whatever family heirlooms she could. Of course, she could never hope to get everything out; the furniture would have to stay, along with a few other bits and pieces. Many things were loaded onto a few wagons. But not about to simply abandon what was left behind to an unknown fate, Henrietta started digging. In a letter to an unnamed family member written shortly after the war, Henrietta described how she, like so many others at the time, had taken to burying silver, jewelry and whatever else around Wantoot's grounds. Two particular 1799 English-made silver pieces—a covered sugar cup and cream pitcher—actually served as containers for smaller items. "Various methods were resorted to save jewelry and other valuables," she wrote. "Among others, I just took a silver cup and filled it with rings, watches, etc. and buried it just below the middle of the bottom step as I sat there."[74]

Just what the Macbeths lost when soldiers did indeed pillage and burn the home still cannot be quantified, but at least Henrietta's endeavors to protect what she could were not in vain. Returning to a charred plantation some months later, she recovered her buried silver and jewelry right where she left them.[75]

At about the same time Henrietta was digging holes, Mary Fripp Tennent and her husband, William, were prudently burying their own silver a short distance away from Parnassus, their plantation home near Goose Creek. For William, a successful merchant and brick manufacturer who spent most of his prewar years securing lucrative government contracts for supplying bricks by the boatload for the Congress-approved construction of Fort Sumter, the precautions proved warranted. Yankee soldiers vengefully sought out his beloved Parnassus and burned it to the ground—a sad twist of irony, really, since the same government that had been William's best customer before secession and the source of much of his wealth was now destroying the symbol of that prosperity.[76]

It took William and Mary Tennent two full years after the war's end to discover the ultimate fate of their home and left-behind belongings. They returned to Parnassus only to find practically nothing left of it—or nothing above ground anyway. Perusing the mess that was once their cherished plantation, Mary stoically scouted out their silver's hiding places and

Silver sugar bowl and cream pitcher (marked by London silversmiths Peter and Ann Bateman in 1799) buried by Henrietta Macbeth at Wantoot Plantation in 1865. *Courtesy of the Charleston Museum.*

Silver service (unmarked) buried by William and Mary Tennant at Parnassus Plantation in 1865. *Courtesy of the Charleston Museum; photo by Charlotte Crabtree.*

successfully excavated every last piece. William sold the ruined property in 1867, but the silver stayed in the family for generations.[77]

Although some might call Henrietta Macbeth's and Mary Tennent's actions innovative, the burial or otherwise concealment of family goods was, in truth, nothing new. In fact, among those families living in the paths of enemy troops during both the Revolutionary and Civil Wars, physically burying wealth was more rule than exception. "The inhabitants of Carolina in general buried their [silver] plate," wrote one Charlestonian, "thinking it a safer depositum…and by preferring this method of concealment, they have all secured their effects." Referring to her now celebrated diary as a "yellow Confederate quire of paper," Mary Boykin Chestnut recorded that not even her thoughts on paper were safe. Explaining in April 1865 her failure to write for three days, Mary revealed the burial of her journal, together with "the silver sugar-dish, teapot, milk-jug, and a few spoons and forks that follow my fortunes as I wander."[78]

For those who wished to press their luck, on the other hand, hoping against hope that the enemy would simply pass by their homes as well as themselves, it was often a losing proposition. An indefensible estate—abandoned or not—put nearly everything up for grabs and at the whims of the soldiery, and it was these men, both friend and foe, who seemingly had an uncanny knack for nastiness. In sacking Henry Laurens's elegant Mepkin Plantation, for instance, redcoats, for no other reason than just the "pure cruelty of it," took the deceased Mrs. Laurens's shoes and further helped themselves to clothing belonging to Colonel Isaac Motte's toddlers.[79]

Just as anxious as everyone else on James Island upon hearing various rumors of rampaging Brits, Joseph Dill Jr. hoped to avoid the redcoats during their march on Charleston. However, with his Dill's Bluff Plantation situated along New Town Creek, a narrow tributary connecting the Stono and Ashley Rivers, he knew his odds of staying clear of their advancement were not good. As foreseen, the Brits landed on James Island in late February 1780 but, much to Dill's relief, headed north up the Ashley River to begin crossing over to the Charleston peninsula. This position, well northwest of Dill's Bluff, kept Joseph and his family out of harm's way—but, alas, not for long. Much to his disappointment, Dill soon learned of a separate force of Hessian grenadiers marching south and east across New Town Creek on their way to Fort Johnson, near the mouth of the harbor, with his plantation right in their path.[80]

Having practically no time to make any sort of serious preparations, there was little Joseph could do to protect his home and belongings from

Silver cruet set with cobalt glass bottles (maker's mark illegible) buried by Joseph and Susannah Dill at Dill's Bluff Plantation in 1780. *Courtesy of the Charleston Museum.*

the oncoming Hessians. Nevertheless, he and his wife, Susannah, feverishly took whatever valuables were within reach—an elegant coin-silver castor set with cobalt glass bottles among them—and began hastily burying them in the nearby gardens. The Dills were lucky. In what would end up being a rare instance of uneventful interaction, the Hessians barely broke stride upon reaching his house, marching hurriedly onward toward Fort Johnson with no time for selfish exploits.[81]

Sadly, various safeguards undertaken by folks like the Dills succeeded only about half the time during the Revolution and even less during the Civil War. In fact, when redcoats finally took Charleston, there was a great, although certainly unsanctioned, effort among the soldiery to seek out concealed goods. Many search parties uncovered "from buried stores" large collections of "plunder in silver plate...merchandise, tobacco, etc." During the Civil War, Charlestonians, including Mary Whilden, were indubitably aware of just how visceral that vengefulness was among the Union's undisciplined rank-and-file, and like so many others, she rushed to protect her home and belongings. Fortunately, her endeavors paid off when two soldiers from the Twenty-first Illinois regiment walked through the front door without so much as a knock. Composed yet defiant, Mary calmly served the pair supper and even halfheartedly apologized for her lack of tableware, later stating, "I had but one spoon visible, and told them they would have to stir their coffee by turns. They seemed to doubt my assertion, and on urging, I told them truthfully, I had sent such articles of value as could be conveniently removed to a place of safety...One looked significantly at the other, saying, 'She acted wisely.'"[82]

Would-be enemy plunderers understood the burial game just as well as the civilians did, and by late 1864, unfortunately, they appeared to expect it. Soldiers commonly took to using bayonets, sabers or other tools to probe gardens, haystacks and even privies in an attempt to discover hidden spoils, and any evidence of freshly stirred soil practically guaranteed a second look, if not an all-out excavation. In exploring the grounds at Eutaw Plantation, for example, Union privates unearthed thirty-four chests of buried goods and proceeded to have a virtual field day with their newfound booty. They were reportedly seen "dressing themselves in the beautiful silks and ornaments taken from the chests" and dancing "gaily about the lawn."[83]

Still choosing to bury her seventy-piece English porcelain table service despite knowing the enemy's penchant for snooping, Mrs. William Jeffords of Charleston added her own brand of insurance against losing it to the Yankee army. Plowing out a rectangular plot in her yard, she buried her

Sketch from *Beadles Magazine* depicting soldiers searching out buried valuables in 1864. *Public domain.*

Portion of Mrs. William Jeffords's English-made, semi-porcelain "cabbage-patch china." *Courtesy of the Charleston Museum.*

goods deep within it, only then proceeding to plant cabbages over them. As expected, troops moved through some days later but, for whatever reason, never gave a second thought to Jeffords's freshly planted garden—even though it was February. Thus, Mrs. Jeffords's vegetable-garden camouflage was a resounding success, and all of her "cabbage-patch china" survives to this very day.[84]

Not so much clever as lucky, Charleston-born Reverend Paul Trapier, a professor at the Episcopal Theological Seminary, narrowly escaped being robbed blind in 1865. With his Camden home essentially surrounded by encamped "marauders who were to be soon among us," Trapier crept silently with his wife, son and nephew into the cellar, where in total darkness they "endeavored to hide in the ground the silver [and] jewels." Sure enough, at daybreak, Yankees entered the residence and "crowded accordingly into the basement of the house…They evidently suspected that we had silver there, for they thrust their bayonets down as deep as they could into the sand at the bottom of it & did in fact come within a few inches of a box containing the chief part of our silver which [we] had buried there."[85]

Probably the worst example of this specific type of treasure hunting came at the expense of Alfred Manigault. A member of Company K, Fourth South Carolina Cavalry, he had fallen dreadfully ill in 1863 and continually struggled with fevers over the following year and a half. Finally, in January 1865, defying both his physician's and family's requests, he returned to his post, serving in the defense of Columbia. His valiance notwithstanding, Manigault within weeks fell violently ill with fever and turbulent hallucinations. He was immediately ambulanced out of harm's way, making it as far as Winnsboro before succumbing to what was later diagnosed as cerebrospinal meningitis. For those accompanying him, there was little choice and even less time for interment. Making use of nearby St. John's Episcopal Church, they buried him coffinless in the adjacent graveyard.[86]

What happened the following day was detestable. Writing a letter to Alfred's brother, Louis, on the tenth anniversary of his brother's death, Edward Horlbeck disclosed just what Federal soldiers had done at the burial site, desecrating not only his grave but his remains as well. Arriving at Winnsboro and passing by St. John's on February 21, Yankees noticed the loose soil of a freshly filled plot and, seeing no sort of grave marker, deduced that the church was attempting to hide its silver. Finding Alfred's body instead, Yankee troops were still no less amused. Removing it from the ground and propping it upright, the soldiers "put a potato in his mouth, while

Alfred Manigault, circa 1855. *Private collection.*

others carried the organ out of the church to play music and dance around it." Concluding his horrific letter to Louis, Horlbeck noted mournfully that, as the enemy was clearly not interested in cleaning up their dirty work, they "took the body and left the Citizens to bury it again."[87]

For the Manigaults, trouble with the enemy was a family tradition of sorts. In 1780, Alfred's grandfather Gabriel surrendered with the rest of the Charleston garrison but at least received a parole pass that "secured him and his property from being molested." If only the same were true for the rest of the family.[88]

During the Civil War, again and again, Louis Manigault had to determine what was valuable, what was worth saving. But his first instinct was the most telling. In what he called his "War Journal," he had the remarkable foresight to transcribe vast reams of his family correspondences—wills, tax statements, receipts and random bits of ephemera—dating all the way back to his colonial forebears of the seventeenth century. His motivation for taking this time-consuming task was simple for him: he was not about to let the Civil War erase his extensive family history.

A privileged lad to say the least, Louis had no plans to curtail his family's successful mercantile and agricultural endeavors. Having traveled and studied extensively, he was ready to settle down in the 1830s and, upon receiving Gowrie Plantation as a gift from his father, was most eager to add to his already sprawling agricultural holdings.[89]

Louis's salad days at Gowrie could not last, however, and the onset of war was likely an especially hard time for him emotionally. Unable to serve the Confederacy due to a prior injury suffered in China, he could only watch as both of his brothers went off to fight, while contenting himself with the management of family's fortunes and the operations at Gowrie. In this, fortuitously, Louis was no dope. He spent the first two years of the war contemplating Yankee raids both in the country and in Charleston, writing feverishly about his family properties in proximity to Federal troops at Port Royal Sound and Hilton Head Island. Yankee scouting and foraging party incursions into Edisto and Johns Islands were only further cause for his concern, and he soon began taking somewhat aggressive measures in relocating family valuables to Augusta:

> *As the situation in Charleston was becoming serious, it was deemed advisable to remove from the city to a locality of greater safety, some of the more precious articles…in the Winter drawing room of our family residence Number 6 Gibbes Street…We have brought to Augusta some furniture and*

many household effects, and my Father has sent me the valuable family silver, &c. My wife's costly portrait is here, with my own...Most probably this shall be our residence until peace is declared, or until all danger of attacking Charleston shall have subsided. Thus as regards as our (Gowrie) property, all at present is uncertain. We have taken every precaution, yet the Enemy are quite near at hand and no one can tell what is yet in store to befall us.[90]

On Christmas Eve 1864, Louis found out.

To say Union troops destroyed Gowrie would be an understatement when, instead, they all but erased it from the map. "The Change in the appearance of Gowrie Settlement is, I may say, from a Village to a Wilderness," Louis observed. The main house, servant house and barn were all burned clean to the ground. Astonishingly, not even the bricks remained, having all been "stolen by the Negroes and sold in Savannah." The contents of the mill—some ten thousand bushels of rice—had disappeared, as had the mill itself, while every field hand, mule, horse and farm animal was gone. Adding insult to injury, Louis sadly remarked that the enemy had not just laid waste to his dwellings; they had even gone so far as to indelibly scar the land itself.

About One Hundred Trees, most of which were "Water Oaks," transplanted in 1852 with my own hands, adorned this Settlement. I had also after numerous attempts finally succeeded in transplanting in 1853 a most beautiful Cypress Tree which stood in front of the House...In 1864 this Cypress was about Thirty feet in height, and most perfect in form. Another handsome tree in this Settlement was a "Sycamore" given me by Mr Joseph Washburn. In 1864 this tree was about forty feet high, and growing most rapidly...For besides the trees the labor of Twelve years had created a flower Garden, well stocked with choice Roses brought from the Nurseries of Charleston and Savannah. The beautiful green "Ivy" encircled the entire brick foundation of the House, whilst the Mutta flora Rose and its white flower Vine grew luxuriantly upon the fences. Of all the above: Trees, Plants, Shrubs, Fences, not a vestige remained, not even the stumps of the trees being visible, all had been used as fire-wood.[91]

As his postwar writings further reveal, Louis's losses did not end with those at Gowrie. Enemy soldiers visited several other family plantations, including Silk Hope on the Cooper River, from which were lifted some wholly irreplaceable, if not unusual, items that, as Louis would later come

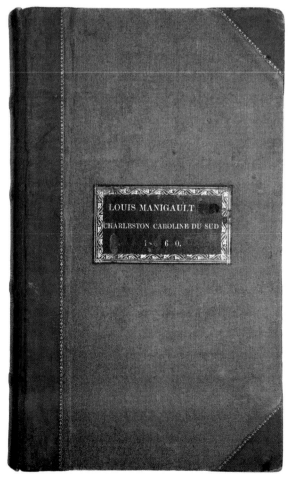

Above: Gowrie Plantation, sketched from memory by Louis Manigault, circa 1880. *Courtesy of the Charleston Museum.*

Left: Louis Manigault's "War Journal," 1860. *Private Collection; photo by Sean Money.*

to learn, were brought back into Charleston and peddled off among the soldiers as souvenirs. Of particular note was a box of "curiosities…collected by my father in foreign countries and were of but little value to others." These included ancient coins, African coral and even an Egyptian mummy's severed hand.[92]

Yet despite the Manigaults' losses, many things, including family portraits, porcelains, silver and jewelry, remained, thanks in part to Louis's fortitude in protecting what he could when he did. Best of all, the Yankees at least never got their hands on Louis's War Journal, and it survives even now as a veritable treasure-trove of family data.

> *Although my valuable library of Historical Works and Books of Travels has been destroyed upon the Plantation…by the Cruel hand of War; and Although my other losses are felt in numerous ways, yet should I render up my sincerest thanks to Almighty God for preserving me this Volume. Experiencing many hair-breath escapes in accompanying me from point to point; causing me uneasiness and deep anxiety; Yet at the Conclusion of our four long years of fearful War it remains intact and safe in my possession.*[93]

Like Louis Manigault, Francis Simons Holmes, Charleston Museum curator, was not one to wait around either, especially once Union artillerists began shelling the city in August 1863. With the museum's vast holdings in significant danger, Holmes urgently began the daunting task of cataloging, packing and moving its collection out of town as fast as humanly possible.

Thankfully, it was suggested to Holmes that, although convenient, his preferred destination in Columbia might not be the wisest of hiding places for the museum holdings, and perhaps he should find someplace a bit more secluded. Heeding this advice, he called on an old friend, George A. Trenholm, who, having acquired Darby Plantation in Edgefield, South Carolina, the year before, had begun covertly using it as a supply depot of sorts, storing fabric, food and saltpeter (the main ingredient in gunpowder) for Confederate use. Ordering that "the cases be sent by rail to Aiken and wagoned thence about twenty miles," Holmes arranged for Trenholm to receive the Charleston Museum's entire collection—over two hundred sealed wooden crates, including invaluable natural history specimens collected by Mark Catesby, Lewis and Clark, John Bachman and John James Audubon. Arriving at Darby, Holmes supervised the stacking and covering of each crate in an outbuilding. Though a small fire ruined Holmes's personal books and notes, along with a few crates, most everything else remained safe until the

Preserved bat specimens collected circa 1840 by John James Audubon and John Bachman, who used them for their descriptions and artwork before placing them in the Charleston Museum's collection. *Courtesy of the Charleston Museum.*

HOME AGAIN.—We congratulate the citizens of Charleston on the safe return of a large portion of that extensive and valuable collection of Natural History belonging to the Museum. Of about two hundred large and well packed cases which had been sent away for safety, only three or four were lost, they were unfortunately destroyed by fire with Prof HOLMES' library. In a few weeks the Museum will be ready to receive visitors, though it must be many months before the collection which contains several thousand specimens, can be possibly relabelled and arranged.

The *Charleston Daily News* announced the return of the Charleston Museum's collection on January 11, 1866. *Courtesy of the Charleston Museum.*

war's end and was finally returned unscathed in 1866 to the accompaniment of much fanfare.[94]

For the general Charleston populace—those without resources or connections—the removal and safeguarding of family valuables was far easier said than done during both wars. Luckily, though, there were options. Just as Henrietta Macbeth had mentioned "various methods" of concealment, home-front families wishing to keep their things from becoming war prizes sometimes had to improvise—and fast. "Let them have that gilt thing!" yelped Godard Bailey in what might be best described as a masterful stroke of reverse psychology as Yankees rummaged through Mulberry Plantation. One soldier, having pocketed a precious gold card case, fell for Bailey's ruse and discarded it on a table, thinking it not nearly as valuable as it actually was.[95]

Occasionally, just hard-nosed defiance was enough. One particular letter from Sarah Lowndes to her husband, Rawlins, dated May 17, 1780, wonderfully exhibits the intuition of a wise woman. Warning Rawlins it was not safe for him to travel homeward since "the Country is so infested with plundering parties," Sarah wrote that "a large party came here yesterday, they said with order to plunder, but [I] told them I was convinced they had no such orders and they should have nothing from me…so I dismissed them." Having had their ridiculous bluff called, it appears that the soldiers acquiesced to Lowndes's demands and simply left. Sarah closed her letter by stating, "We are all well here and happy."[96]

Finally, there are a scattered few invigorating—if not inspirational—examples of protection by the unlikeliest of champions. John Deas, whose rice plantation stood some twenty miles north of Charleston, had certainly heard a multitude of horror stories concerning the redcoats. Despite this, however, he decided that, come what may, he would not abandon his home. Thus, when two overbearing British colonels loudly arrived at his front door in the winter of 1781, he calmly accepted his fate. Expecting to be either roughed up, robbed, burned out or possibly all three, Deas calmly allowed the pair inside, whereupon he immediately realized that this was going to be a most unusual house call.

One of the two officers had fallen quite ill, and the other was visibly concerned for his compatriot's health. Deas and his wife immediately made the two comfortable for the night, drying their clothes, feeding them and providing suitable quarters, where each could rest peacefully for as long as needed. Presenting themselves as Colonels Doyle and Watson, the pair awoke the following morning in decent enough shape to continue on their way.

The following year, Deas once again received an unexpected visit from the two colonels, who had returned to pay their overdue debt. In defeat, British garrisons outside Charleston were making their way into the city for an orderly evacuation. However, explaining that "a retreating army is always more or less mischievous," the officers had purposely sought out Deas and his wife to "prevent any of their stragglers from plundering or molesting a family that had received them with so much kindness and hospitality a year before."[97]

V

THE PURSUIT OF PROVISIONS

From the Union army's "Special Field Orders No. 120," November 9, 1864:

> *IV. The army will forage liberally on the country during the march. To this end, each brigade commander will organize a good and sufficient foraging party, under the command of one or more discreet officers, who will gather, near the route traveled, corn or forage of any kind, meat of any kind, vegetables, corn-meal, or whatever is needed by the command, aiming at all times to keep in the wagons at least ten days' provisions for the command and three days' forage. Soldiers must not enter the dwellings of the inhabitants, or commit any trespass, but during a halt or a camp they may be permitted to gather turnips, apples, and other vegetables, and to drive in stock of their camp.*
>
> *VI. As for horses, mules, wagons, &c., belonging to the inhabitants, the cavalry and artillery may appropriate freely and without limit, discriminating, however, between the rich, who are usually hostile, and the poor or industrious, usually neutral or friendly. Foraging parties may also take mules or horses to replace the jaded animals of their trains, or to serve as pack-mules for the regiments or brigades. In all foraging, of whatever kind, the parties engaged will refrain from abusive or threatening language, and may, where the officer in command thinks proper, give written certificates of the facts, but no receipts, and they will endeavor to leave with each family a reasonable portion for their maintenance.*[98]

Of all that was wrong with the victimization of Charleston's home front during its wars, military commanders and the historians who study them have continually debated the unfortunate, albeit necessary, act of foraging—in other words, the continual effort to keep troops supplied, fed and mobile. Now, as ethically questionable as foraging might seem in retrospect, the whole object of a marching army was indeed lost if it could not sustain itself. At the very least, the men had to eat. Not even Pierre Beauregard could deny his archenemy Quincy Gillmore the necessity of foraging and even told him so on July 4, 1863. Going so far as to reference Swiss diplomat Emer de Vattel's 1760 Law of Nations, in a letter to Gillmore, Beauregard made clear the line between forgivable forage and pitiless pillage. Deeming the latter as "savage and monstrous excess," he still almost politely left the door open to his enemy's want of food and other basics. "You may indeed," he wrote, "waste and destroy provisions and forage which you cannot carry away, and which, if left, would materially assist the operations of your enemy."[99]

So, in the not uncommon event that commissariats or quartermasters could not deliver even meager necessities, what, exactly, was OK to take, what was not and, furthermore, who could really judge between the two? More importantly, in the gathering of food and supplies, could officers realistically draw a hard line between their soldiers' search for provisions and their penchant for plundering? In South Carolina's case, usually not. Nevertheless, for both sides during both wars, foraging was an obligatory, if not critical, exercise in upholding the overall fighting strength of the soldiery. As Clara Barton noted, "Every civilized government is financially able to provide for its armies, but the great and seemingly insuperable difficulty is, to always have what is wanted at the place where it is most needed."[100]

Foraging was oftentimes unavoidable, thanks in large part to the sheer logistical nightmare of keeping troops on their feet. While there were a scattered few attempts to avoid foraging's slippery slope, the success of such attempts were dubious at best. Among the Brits, in fact, there was a time-honored belief that foraging was an ill-advised last resort, fraught with danger. King Richard II's 1385 Articles of War, for example, specifically forbade soldiers from foraging, warning that any man taking even basic provisions "for the refreshment of the army" would be punished "on pain of losing his head." General Henry Clinton, to his credit, loathed foraging for no other reason than it practically always led to greater crimes. He was right. Desertion and looting prevailed among these parties, and far worse, their typically insolent aggression only further angered the Americans—especially those who until then had remained impartial, even sympathetic, to the British cause. As

Union Foragers by Winslow Homer, 1863. *Library of Congress.*

General William Moultrie observed, the "ill treatment" of British and Tory soldiers "soon…obliged them to break their engagements to the British, and to resume their arms, and join the Americans."[101]

For both British and American forces in 1779, most understood that given their respective circumstances, foraging was, for lack of a better term, permissible. Though British quartermaster and commissary departments had been in operation for nearly a century before the American Revolution, neither seemed prepared to handle the massive needs of fighting a large-scale war thousands of miles from home. By the time of their 1778 southern campaign, food estimates were consistently short, and ration deliveries continually failed to adequately meet what was actually required. As a result, enemy foraging in the Carolina Lowcountry by 1779 had become nothing less than a mandatory measure for a soldier's survival.[102]

Of course, whatever problems the redcoats were having paled in comparison to those of their American adversaries. In his memoirs, Henry Lee recalled how meat had become nothing short of a delicacy during his legion's 1781 march from Orangeburg to Eutaw Springs, with his men resorting to eating frogs and the occasional alligator for sustenance. Furthermore, as the *South Carolina Weekly Gazette* reported on March 29, 1783, the lack of governmental support made it nearly impossible for provisions to keep pace with troop movements. It noted how

> *the soldiers were driven to beg their bread, and plunder the markets, against every effort of their officers to prevent it…What is an officer to do with his troops? Congress cannot support them…The State in which they serve, it is said, are under no obligations to support them…This is in fact saying that troops ought to starve unless the general has the power of creating loaves and fishes to feed them on.*[103]

By the 1860s, the jaw-dropping spectacles of massive military wagon trains proved at least somewhat more effective, to be sure, but still was not without its flaws. Mold, rodents, insects and other vermin wreaked havoc on food stores, and soggy weather constantly rotted corn and grain. If, or more like when, wagons broke down, troops were needed to guard the cargos from "bushwhackers" and other small bands of guerrilla raiders while their entire contents were unloaded and redistributed. Slowing things up even more, wagons, carts and caissons loaded down with small-arms ammunition and ordnance—extremely heavy and cumbersome loads of lead, iron and gunpowder—took priority at the front of the line and put the entire train at the mercy of the heaviest vehicles' speed. Still, upward of five thousand wagons accompanied Sherman's southern crusade at one time or another, and before commencing his South Carolina campaign, he requested that, for a single corps, three hundred wagons were needed for twenty days' worth of food and another three hundred for ammunition, clothing and "other necessary stores." Add to this a substantial herd of beef cattle following along on the hoof, and a single line of troops, artillery caissons, wagons and livestock could easily stretch out some sixty miles or more, providing Carolina towns with some of the most horrific traffic jams of the nineteenth century. Catherine McLaurin, a disheartened observer in Sumter County, noted how even the "lengthy" train from one of Sherman's smaller detachments "took several hours" to pass by.[104]

Obviously, keeping thousands of soldiers healthy was a daunting task, no matter what was readily at hand. "The soldiers are always willing to bear the largest measure of privation," recalled Sherman. "Probably no army ever had a more varied experience in this regard than the one I commanded in 1864–'65." Thus, in order to supplement their wagon trains and avoid the total collapse of their forces, enemy officers routinely sent out their forage parties, fully aware of their inability to prevent depredations.[105]

Of course, what actually fit into the category of forage was entirely dependent on the instigator's personal point of view—a perspective usually falling somewhere beyond the bounds of propriety. As alluded to previously, foragers on either side had no trouble morphing effortlessly from food gatherers to straight-up thieves. In 1781, for example, Arthur Middleton lost his prized racehorse, Babraham, to foraging Tories, who, although in need of horses, likely singled that one out deliberately due to both malevolence and pecuniary value. Upon reaching the Ponpon River near Edisto that same year, Alexander Chesney, a Loyalist serving under Lord Rawdon, casually wrote of his troops' necessary procurement of numerous feather beds, not for their comfort but instead to "transport those who could not swim across." Eliza Wilkinson, meanwhile, received yet another visit from a foraging party, who, besides taking food and animals, proceeded to dismantle the house itself for firewood and other resources. "Again plundered, worse than ever plundered!" she bemoaned. "Our very doors and window-shutters were taken from the house…the sashes beaten out; furniture demolished; goods carried off; beds ripped up; stock of every kind driven away; in short, distress of every nature attended us."[106]

The small herd of water buffalo at Middleton Place—the first of its kind in the nation—provides an additional example of an enemy forager's subjectivity. Williams Middleton had traveled much of the world by the 1830s, during which time he saw his first water buffalo at work and understood immediately the benefits one might bring to his already thriving rice plantations back home. For sure, the beasts were near perfect tools for the job: their wide hooves moved well in deep mud without sticking, they seemingly had no fear of water even when up to their eyeballs in it and, above all, their enormous size and strength would make quick work of tilling swampy, low-lying rice fields. After inheriting Middleton Place, Williams spared no expense in procuring a number of water buffalo, shipping them all the way from Constantinople and continuing to raise them into the 1860s.[107]

Having never before laid eyes on such creatures, it is unclear exactly how Union troops from the Fifty-sixth New York Regiment reacted upon discovering the eleven enormous "water bulls" at Middleton Place on February 22, 1865. But regardless of their novelty or necessity, they were fair game. Williams was not around to watch as Federal troops lay waste to his house, nor was he there to see six of his imported water buffalo butchered and eaten by his enemies. Those not consumed on the spot were simply "driven off," their ultimate fate remaining a mystery until sometime around 1870, when Williams somehow learned that three were, in fact, living comfortably in New York's Central Park Zoo, each a "gift" from General Quincy Gillmore.[108]

Understandably miffed, Williams endeavored to recover his unique livestock but remained skeptical about the possibility of success. Soliciting aid from his first cousin Jane Lynch Pringle, a prominent New Yorker, Williams wrote on September 27, 1870, "I do not know how to set about this…It appears to me probable that through your friendly intercourse with the many of the most distinguished citizens of N.Y. some one or two might be found through whose influence the city council, or the Regents of the Park, might be induced to restore me my property or at least its value."[109]

Alas, the two made little headway. Finally, as a last-ditch effort, Williams wrote to city official W.D. Clancy, who audaciously refused to believe the family claims that the park's buffalo were stolen property. Williams angrily rebutted Clancy's ridiculous skepticism by reminding him that, first of all, water buffalo were not exactly the most common animals in America, and secondly, his own son had recognized at least two of them during his last trip to New York. On November 29, 1870, he wrote, "I beg leave to say that there can be but little question as to [the water buffalo's] identity [since] no one in lower S. Carolina except myself had any…My son subsequently saw and recognized some of them at the Central Park in N.Y. two years ago—a bull and a cow in particular, whose shoulder had been scorched…" Regrettably, Clancy and others ignored Williams Middleton's numerous pleas for the safe return of his remaining water buffalo. He never saw them again.[110]

Of course, livestock—exotic or not—was just one commodity among countless other "essentials" sought by foragers. Alcohol was another notoriously ubiquitous "necessity" that, for soldiers and their superiors, fell into an always-questionable gray area. On one hand, medical personnel needed it as a pain reliever for the wounded and a tonic for the well. On the other, it was, according to some, the root of all evil—as unwelcome in camp as the plague. Whatever the need, though, be it fundamental forage or self-satisfaction, wine, ale, brandy and whiskey were eagerly sought by everyone.[111]

Long instilled in Charles Manigault's French Huguenot heritage was a refined taste for only the best Madeira. So much so, in fact, that between 1820 and 1830, he had accumulated a whopping 800 bottles of it. Another large purchase in 1838 added 1,300 more of, as Charles put it, "the finest Madeira wine ever imported in this city, by ship *Belvidera*…which I bottled myself and placed it during twenty-two years under a hot shingled roof." By late 1860, Charles was wholly displeased with the uncontrollable conditions of his own garret and decided it best to move all 2,100 bottles to a somewhat safer environ—another of his properties, the old Powder Magazine on Cumberland Street. Built in 1713 (and still standing today as Charleston's oldest public building), it was actually perfect for wine storage. Its three-foot-thick brick walls and sand-packed roof provided a stable temperature, its boarded windows kept the inside in perpetual darkness and, perhaps most importantly, its strong doors and gates could provide adequate security for the expensive stash. Charles's son Louis would later transcribe from his father's writings that after an initial transport of 800 bottles, the remaining cache was moved on November 5:

> [I] *now transport* [the remaining 1,300 bottles] *to a shelved closet made purposely for it in the old magazine. Previous to this, there was in the magazine (as stated by my Father using his exact words), as follows:*

Bought from Mr. Redmond, Importers here by Mr. Jonathan Lucas in 1830	*410*
Bought from McNeil & Blair. Been two voyages to East Indies for the benefit of the heat as ballast	*170*
Given me by Mr. Nathaniel Heyward, bottled by him in 1823	*50*
Old Family wine, bottled in Philadelphia 1820	*70*
Old Family Wine, various dates, from Philadelphia 1827	*100*
	800 btls.[112]

Circa 1864 "Cattle Raid" sketch by Alfred Waud depicting General Wade Hampton III's men confiscating cattle near Coggins Point, Virginia. *Library of Congress.*

With his extraordinary collection now secured and an inventory completed, Charles made final plans for his wine, instructing that all 2,100 bottles were "to be divided equally among my children at my death." They never got the chance. In January 1864, city authorities stumbled across a very drunk Confederate soldier, slumped practically unconscious outside the magazine door. It appeared that even though the building was holding fast in the face of war, its locks were not. Consequently, it was strongly recommended to Charles that perhaps he should check on his wine.[113]

Charles needed only two small carts to remove what was left of his once famous Madeira collection from the Powder Magazine, transporting the remaining bottles to an out-of-town family farm. As Charles's son Gabriel would write some years later, with indiscriminate Union shelling having driven most Charleston citizens away en masse the previous year, "it was no longer possible to prevent this precious wine from being stolen...The contents of the Cumberland Magazine began to diminish night after night."[114]

While locals could live without luxuries like silver, art, furniture and, yes, probably even Madeira, to have their livestock and produce taken from them presented an entirely new and certainly more serious set of problems. Indeed, food taken for soldiers, enemy or not, was food taken from civilians. By doing so, foragers left homesteaders to starve, thus committing perhaps the worst possible crime. Occasionally, it seems that even the enemy paused long enough to consider this particular outcome. Observing "conduct so atrocious," Major John André noted that more often than not, most victims of forage and the plundering that usually accompanied it were not people of means who could absorb being robbed of the necessities for their very survival. Furthermore, one Union officer wrote home in 1865 that while there was "considerable excitement in foraging," it was a "disagreeable business…to go into people's houses and take their provisions and have the women begging and entreating you to leave a little when you are necessitated to take all." That same year, worried not simply for his family's livelihood but instead for their very lives, Thomas B. Ferguson petitioned Union general

Sherman's Bummers Foraging in South Carolina. From *Frank Leslie's Illustrated Newspaper,* June 17, 1865. *Library of Congress.*

John P. Hatch to return at least some of the seven thousand rice bushels that Yankee soldiers had removed from his father's Berkeley County plantation. To his dismay, he later learned that while over one thousand bushels had been sent downriver to Bennett's Rice Mill in Charleston, not a single grain from the other six thousand could be accounted for.[115]

For obvious reasons, Confederate troops did not take kindly to their enemy's foraging and, considering it nothing less than cold-blooded freebooting among the North's left-behind, deserter types, were more than quick on the trigger when happening upon them. As such, Union troops working separately—that is, away from their army's main body—did so at extreme risk to themselves, no matter their intentions. Myriad accounts of slaughtered Yankee foragers in South Carolina are not overly difficult to find in the annals of state war history. Clearly, as far as most Southerners were concerned anyway, whatever marginal difference existed between official Federal foragers and rogue Yankee pillagers was of no importance, and it was these "bummers," as Carolinians called them, who seemed the most dangerous of bandits. One 1866 publication described them as "a party of foragers on their way out of the lines…who are out thus early in order to carry out their motto, of 'primitias corripere'; and believe most fully in the advantages of early rising, to enable them to gather the first fruits—i.e., first plucking of any house."[116]

Angered by Union bummers, who regularly mixed foraging with plundering, the Charleston Light Dragoons, one of the earliest and most elite volunteer mounted militias, with membership drawn from many of Charleston's most celebrated families, took action. The Dragoons had mustered several times during the antebellum period, including the Nullification Crisis and the Mexican-American War, each time acquitting themselves admirably as a well-organized and well-trained cavalry. It was in the waning stages of the Civil War, however, that the once exclusive, upper-echelon gentlemen of the Dragoons began their spiraling descent into savagery, spending many a day running down and killing as many bummers as they could find as "a source for sport."[117]

The Dragoons had certainly seen better days by 1865. Devastated by the battles of Matadequin Creek, Trevilian Station and especially Haw's Shop, where they had "stood still to be shot down in their tracks, having no orders to retire," what was left of the proud unit, now tattered and broken, limped back to South Carolina just in time to see Charleston and Columbia overrun by the Feds. Their numbers too few to attack any of the Union's formal detachments, the Dragoons set their sights on softer targets instead, primarily Yankee foragers and bummers.[118]

One rather grisly run-in occurred at "Cantey's plantation," near the southern end of Florence County. On the morning of February 26, scouts reported seeing enemy foragers "loading eight or ten wagons from Mr. Cantey's barns" and immediately recognized their advantage because so long as loot was in their hands, their guns were not. Indeed having "stacked their arms in the yard," said the scouts, "you can bag every one of them." Riding as quietly as possible, the Dragoons dismounted and approached to "within a few yards of the house."[119]

It happened fast and was over quick. Before the Federals could react, a wall of Dragoon gunfire and slashing sabers made "quick clean work." While some vainly attempted to retrieve their weapons, the rest panicked and fled unarmed. "Not many escaped," wrote one attacker, "for there were open fields around and behind the house extending a considerable distance, which afforded the cavalry a fair chance for such pell-mell business."[120]

As food and supplies reached an all-time low by the winter of 1865, the Federal army's food-gathering sorties reached an all-time high. These extremities, in turn, presented not just the Charleston Light Dragoons but Confederate defenders in general with opportunities aplenty to impose their own brand of reckoning on the enemy. Carnage permeated the region. Sherman's aide-de-camp George Nichols wrote of men turning up

Feeding 8,000 People with Rations of Rice and Salt at West Point Mills, on the Ashley River. From *Frank Leslie's Illustrated Newspaper*, April 15, 1865. *Courtesy of the Charleston Museum.*

hanged or shot, with notes attached to their clothing reading, "Death to all foragers." Another group of twenty-one infantrymen was found stacked in a ravine, each with his throat slit. Eventually, Sherman took notice. Writing to Lieutenant General Wade Hampton III just days after Charleston's evacuation and Columbia's burning, Sherman surprisingly sympathized with the Rebels—at least sort of. While understanding that his foragers' partiality for pillage was indeed why they were being killed, he was still not about to condone his opponent's shoot-first practices:

> *I have no doubt this is the occasion of much misbehavior on the part of our men, but I cannot permit an enemy to judge or punish with wholesale murder. Personally, I regret the bitter feelings engendered by this war, but they were to be expected, and I simply allege that those who struck the first blow and made war inevitable ought not, in fairness, to reproach us for the natural consequences. I merely assert our war right to forage and my resolve to protect my foragers to the extent of life for life.[121]*

Predictably, Hampton was less than cordial in his response to Sherman's note. At the age of forty-two, the Charleston-born, third-generation warrior had financed his own "Hampton's Legion." During the course of the war, he had already seen one son die and the other wounded by Yankee bullets. Time and time again, he had witnessed how starvation and destitution placed "more than one household [in] agony far more bitter than that of death." Thus for Hampton, whatever Sherman had to complain about was roundly irrelevant. Caring not for Sherman's whining, Hampton wrote back:

> *It is a part of the system of the thieves whom you designate as your foragers to fire the dwellings of those citizens whom they have robbed. To check this inhuman system, which is justly execrated by every civilized nation, I have directed my men to shoot down all of your men who are caught burning houses. This order shall remain in force so long as you disgrace the profession of arms by allowing your men to destroy private dwellings...From my heart*

I wish that every old man and boy in my country who can fire a gun would shoot down, as he would a wild beast, the men who are desolating their land, burning their homes, and insulting their women.[122]

In reality, Lowcountry supplies had been slowly dwindling ever since the 1861 fall of Port Royal. Within the year, Union troop incursions into Wadmalaw and Edisto Islands pushed many planters to burn or otherwise destroy their crops, denying the Yankees any spoils. This, when combined with the pervasive foraging of 1864 and 1865, created shortages on a grand scale, but not until the war was over could Federal officers grasp the magnitude of privation among Charleston's population. By the spring of 1865, occupying Union officials as well as the newly established Freedmen's Bureau were struggling to aid the tens of thousands of destitute and hungry civilian survivors, both white and black. Reconfiguring the West Point rice mill as Charleston's main relief center, they dispensed whatever rations of rice, grist and salt were available.[123]

In their agony, Charlestonians would not soon forget what they, their neighbors and their city endured from one war to the next. The fallout of enemy foraging, turned bumming, turned plundering was seemingly everywhere, as historian Dr. David Ramsay reflected:

In the end…they had spread over a considerable extent of country, and small parties visited almost every house, stripping it of whatever was most valuable, and rifling the inhabitants of their money, rings, jewels, and other personal ornaments…Feather-beds were ripped open for the sake of the ticking. Windows, china-ware, looking glasses and pictures were dashed to pieces. Not only the larger domestic animals were cruelly and wantonly shot down, but the licentiousness of the soldiery extended so far that, in several places, nothing within their reach, however small and insignificant, was suffered to live.[124]

VI

TROUBLE FROM HOME

Although pillage defined how many Charleston civilians experienced the city's military occupations, it was most assuredly not the only element of strife they had to endure. In the face of any crisis, trouble can come from all sides, and as noted earlier, it is an all-around reckless claim to suggest that every calamity Charleston suffered, every heirloom lost, was at the hands of its enemies.

Wartime struggles aside, weather and various manmade misfortunes did excellent jobs of severely diminishing—nigh wiping out—whatever prominence Charleston had established up to that point. The turn of the eighteenth century, for example, should have marked success for the Charles Towne endeavor, but severe fires, crippling spates of disease and a massive hurricane (the storm surge of which pushed a wall of seawater "in upon Charlestown with amazing impetuosity") almost ended the place. A 1698 letter from colonial governor Joseph Blake described the dire situation: "We have had the small-pox amongst us nine or ten months, which hath been very infectious and mortal. We have lost by the distemper 200 or 300 persons…a fire broke out in the night [February 24] in Charles-Town, which hath burnt the dwellings, stores and out-houses, of at least fifty families, and hath consumed in houses and goods, the value of £30,000 sterling."[125]

The colonists slowly recovered and rebuilt, just in time to go through it all again not three years later. This time, fires, storms and sicknesses took even more lives and pushed nearly everyone to consider moving to Pennsylvania:

Few families escaped a share of the public calamities. Almost all were lamenting the loss, either of their habitations by the devouring flames, or of friends or relations by the infectious and loathsome maladies. Discouragement and despair sat on every countenance. Many of the survivors could think of nothing but abandoning a country on which the judgments of heaven seemed to fall so heavy, and in which there was so little prospect of success, heath, or happiness. [We] had heard of Pennsylvania, and how pleasant and flourishing a province it was described to be, and therefore were determined to embrace the first opportunity that offered of retiring to it with the remainder of [our] families and effects.[126]

It is furthermore crucial to note that Charleston has twice burned while at war, each occurrence an unquestionably clear cause for many lost valuables. In 1778, as redcoats put their southern strategy into high gear, fire burned away many of the city's warehouses and shops in less than a day's time. James Munro, a silversmith and jeweler, whose inventory had been looted in the fire's aftermath, used the *South Carolina Gazette* to beseech the return of his merchandise. Additionally, "The Charles Town Library Society's valuable collection of books, instruments and apparatus," wrote William Mazyck, "[was] almost entirely lost."[127]

Of course, the greatest conflagration came on December 11, 1861, not quite a year after South Carolina secession and a mere eight months into the Civil War. The damage was bad. The timing, however, could not have been worse. The Confederacy's need for men had left Charleston fire companies severely short-handed. Making matters so much worse, an extreme low tide drained water levels agonizingly out of the reach of pump hoses. Pushed by wind, the colossal fire produced "a great scar of bare and blackened walls" as it swept violently in a southwesterly path across town, isolating the peninsula's southern tip. Hundreds of local families lost everything of value. The Carolina Art Association, whose 1858 catalogue listed 176 masterpieces dating back to the Temple of Bacchus, lost practically all of its collection, while the Apprentices' Library Society, a school of sorts for the burgeoning craftsmen class, with seven thousand volumes of "the largest and most valuable" works on architecture, collapsed in a heap.[128]

Now, while historians still argue whether Charleston's fire epidemic was preventable, the weather, all can agree, obviously was not. Hurricanes consistently harassed Charlestonians, all of whom spent their summers "in a painful state of anxiety, not knowing what course to pursue nor what is best to be done" in saving their family treasures from ruin.[129]

One poorly timed 1752 storm, which struck during a full-moon high tide, effortlessly hurled large sailing vessels over the sea wall, smashing them into houses. The resulting floodwaters inundated everything. The crop devastation alone left authorities wondering if the city had enough food left to feed its residents. Panic ensued. Looting began. By the time it was all over, Charleston was so stripped bare that its surveyor general had to offer up rewards of fifty pounds to anyone who could locate "any one of [his] books of plats, deeds, and accounts." Disgusted at Charleston's infrastructural breakdown, Governor James Glen took to the *South Carolina Gazette* to publicly shame Charleston's rampant thievery:

> *Having received information that…wicked and ill-disposed Persons, regardless of the laws of God or of the Province, and divesting themselves of all Humanity for their Fellow Subjects, take advantage of the Calamity with which it hath pleased God to afflict the Inhabitants…and go about picking up, purloining and plundering, the Goods, Wares and Merchandize [sic], Household Furniture, Sails, Rigging, Timber, Boards, Shingles, and other Things…in different Parts of Charles Town, and elsewhere; and His Excellency, and the Council, greatly sympathizing with the unhappy Sufferers, and being desirous to protect all His Majesty's subjects…are determined to discourage and prevent…the above abominable and iniquitous Practice.*[130]

Another severe hurricane in 1838 hit Sullivan's Island and annihilated whatever art, silver, ceramics and furniture lay inside the summer homes of Charleston's wealthiest planter families. Charles Manigault recorded his rather bleak assessment the following morning, writing how the integrity of most houses deteriorated so quickly that it "prevented saving their contents… The loss sustained by land and water, we are not at present able to estimate. It cannot be less, however, than $200,000. But the destruction of property is of no consideration, when we think of the loss of lives. Mr. Leval…has been severely wounded by the oversetting of his house, and his wife and children killed…Several dead bodies have been picked up in the river."[131]

Finally, and no less worthy of mention, was the unfamiliar and catastrophic wallop that Charlestonians received in 1886. Though journalists of the eighteenth and nineteenth centuries occasionally mentioned earthquakes, very few residents took serious notice. In 1809, for example, Dr. David Ramsay remarked, "From the fatal consequences of earthquakes, we are happily exempt…Earthquakes in Carolina are harmless." Fortunately for Ramsay, he died long before having to eat his words. On August 31, 1886, with darkness having set in after 9:30 p.m., an earthquake, unprecedented in scale, hit Charleston and near total chaos followed. Colonel J.H. Averill described the terrible damage done to his home and cherished heirloom furnishings: "There came a crash...The lamp and bookcase were overturned, a table seemed to be dancing on the floor and the pictures on the wall appeared to be falling...Chimneys have gone down through the centre of the house, carrying with them mantels, furniture and everything in their way."[132]

Regrettably, even though disasters should account for significant local property losses, neither the size nor severity of such events can compete with what went missing during the city's wartime sieges and subsequent occupations. Culpability for these robberies, however, was widespread. As invoked in the Gospel according to St. John: "He that is without sin...let him cast the first stone." Neither the Patriots, the Confederates nor the townspeople could count themselves blameless when it came to the losses of treasure among their own brethren.[133]

During the American Revolution, homegrown raiders were not uncommon, and commanders in South Carolina were having problems of their own. Taking over General Thomas Sumter's brigade, for example, Colonel William Henderson quickly assessed his new unit as "the most discontented set of men I ever saw, both men and officers...The thirst after plunder that seems to prevail among the soldiery makes the command almost intolerable. This circumstance is most disagreeable, as this infamous practice seems to be countenanced by too many officers." Colonel Wade Hampton I was another who voiced his disgust at larcenous soldiers passing through Lexington County in July 1781:

> *The situation in which I found this neighborhood...is truly to be lamented. Almost every person...seems to have been combined in committing robberies, the most base and inhuman that ever disgrace mankind...The more daring but equally guilty part of this banditti seemed to threaten immediate destruction (by murder, etc) to those who might presume to call the conduct of them or their accomplices into question.*[134]

As for the state of affairs in Charleston, it did not take General Benjamin Lincoln long to recognize that having his soldiers holed up on an urban peninsula was a recipe for trouble, and by the end of 1779, he had prudently put forth orders that he hoped would safeguard residents. For starters, under no circumstances could enlisted men gallivant around town without a pass, and even if they had one, they could use it only during predetermined daylight hours. Lincoln also barred his men from carrying firearms outside their encampment, unless duty-bound to do so, and further stated that no homestead was to be disturbed without permission unless some kind of emergency demanded it. For Lincoln, it was a commendable, albeit unsuccessful, effort. Despite his orders and best intentions, patrols constantly rounded up wayward Patriot soldiers, sometimes catching them with plundered goods from nearby homes.[135]

Only adding to the turmoil were Lincoln's own follies. By March 1780, his stretched nerves were becoming obvious. In one of his more bizarre orders, Lincoln demanded that every dog in Charleston be either killed or thrown out of town, their infernal barking at all hours of the night being "so intolerable that the Soldiers off duty cannot get rest." More concerned that perhaps their unceasing noise was causing unnecessary anxieties, which, in turn, could trigger false alarms of a redcoat attack, Lincoln allowed patrols carte blanche to search alleys, streets, yards and "any House by Day, or Night, to destroy Dogs that may disturb the quiet of the Garrison." One can easily imagine the reactions to Lincoln's decree, but for some less-than-ethical Patriots, it must have been a delight since they could now cite noisy canines as an excuse to enter private properties.[136]

As for domestic looters receiving their due punishment, accounts of such occurrences exist but are expectedly rare. In October 1779, Isaac Wood and a Captain Carter were arrested and court-martialed in Charleston for "plundering contrary to repeated Orders." Carter was cashiered. Wood, conversely, was turned over to civil authorities, who immediately ordered that the "effects taken be returned" to their rightful owners. In many other cases around the Lowcountry, unfortunately, American officers' earnest attempts to quell looting by the enemy and their own men did not succeed. On May 15, 1781, for instance, after defeating British major Andrew Maxwell and taking Fort Granby in Lexington County, Colonel Henry Lee faced a rather strange, albeit sadly unavoidable, decision. In negotiating the surrender of his strategic position, Maxwell brazenly requested that Lee allow both him and his men to go free and keep whatever plunder they had with them. Lee was naturally furious, but with British reinforcements on the way, time was short. He had little choice. As he saw it, capturing Maxwell's position was more important than the man himself, so Lee reluctantly let him leave—with two bulging wagonloads of loot in tow.[137]

For Charlestonians living with national war between 1861 and 1863, giving up goods was a mostly voluntary sacrifice for the good of the

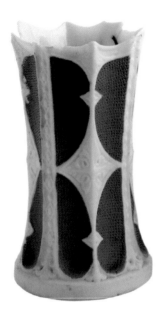
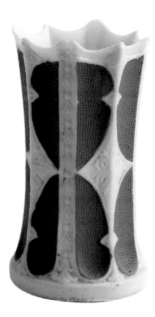

Pair of American bisque-porcelain vases purchased by Charles T. Haskell at an 1863 gunboat fair. Haskell died on Morris Island a few weeks later. *Courtesy of the Charleston Museum.*

Portion of a French porcelain tea service donated as a gunboat raffle prize by Theresa A. McDonald in 1862. *Courtesy of the Charleston Museum.*

Confederate cause. To this end, local supporters often organized fundraising bazaars, raffles, balls and concerts to procure money for military supplies and armaments. "Gunboat fairs" raised money to construct ironclads for the Confederate navy. For these occasions, families gave generously in both money and merchandise. They donated prized possessions. Theresa A. McDonald gave a French tea service. Susan Gelzer offered up a linen folding fan. Mary Chestnut donated "a string of pearls to be raffled for at the Gunboat Fair," while poignantly noting the frivolousness of such heirlooms when lives were at stake: "We do not spare our precious things, no. Our silver and gold, what are they?—when we give up to war our beloved."[138]

Now, while Charlestonians were doing well in giving away their excesses, scores of speedy, streamlined, state-of-the-art blockade runners were doing even better in replenishing their shortages. For the first half of the war, these swift ships repeatedly outran the Federal fleet's attempts to bar their entry as they supplied and resupplied the city with not only war "materiel"—firearms, lead and gunpowder—but also fancy luxuries, including silk, cigars, wine, furniture and fine porcelain. Yet despite their incredible triumphs, blockade runners could do little to prevent blockade-driven inflation. Higher prices were a burden on Charleston's wealthy—and a flat-out crisis for its lower classes. Demand for daily necessities increased exponentially once the Union navy showed up outside Charleston Harbor in 1861, making supplies so tight that even the slightest hiccup sent prices sky high. Certainly not all blockade runners were successful, and the occasional capture of just one or two usually proved a tough loss for both soldiers and noncombatants alike.[139]

Not even generals were immune. In need of a new saddle after his defeat at Shiloh, General Pierre Beauregard paid a Paris firm handsomely for a custom-made pigskin saddle, complete with silver-plated brass bosses cast with the state seal of Louisiana (his home state). Due to the Federal blockade, however, he never received it. Loaded aboard a blockade runner destined for Charleston and New Orleans, the vessel was intercepted by a Yankee gunship, which confiscated all its cargo and sent it north.[140]

It was after Union forces finally gained control of Morris Island in September 1863 that Charleston received its first crippling blow, one that at last presented the city with the rebellion's first real consequences. By summer's end, Federal batteries on the island's landward side were hurling shells into the city. Perhaps worse, their seaward guns now covered the main deepwater channels and instantly slammed the door on Charleston's

The remains of an unidentified blockade runner run aground off Sullivan's Island, circa 1865. *Library of Congress.*

incredibly vital blockade-running enterprise. Thus, with virtually no protection coming from Confederate Charleston, blockade-running captains faced a rather easy decision: either find a safer harbor elsewhere or have their ships, their cargo and themselves blasted into little bits. Hence, for the better part of the following year, only four blockade runners successfully made port in Charleston.[141]

The results of this shutdown were as immediate as they were catastrophic. Basic living conditions deteriorated dramatically. Once tolerable inconveniences morphed into all-out anxieties and soon gave way to pure fear and desperation. Concluding his letter to a friend, Charles Holst made his worries clear: the entire town might soon be starving.

> *It is well my Wife is dead, for suffer we must if this Madd [sic] foolish war last much longer, our Money are [sic] worthless, confidence is lost…Butter [is] $4—Eggs [are] $2, we have a little meat but dare scarsely [sic] use it as no more can be had, some are even worse off than I, [We] cannot get anything to feed Cows or for milk, I will give you my own personal Fare…for Breakfast, a cup of slop or Rye coffee without Sugar, dry corn Bread & no butter, Dinner, a few Eggs either fryed [sic] or boiled & Cow*

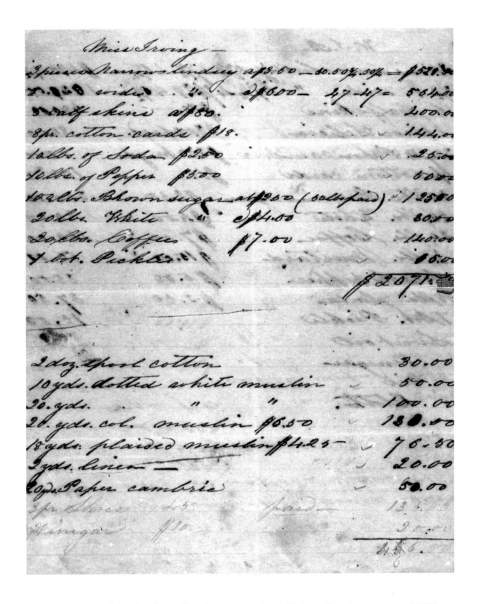

Above: "Ms. Irving's List" reflects Charleston's massive inflation after the summer of 1863. *Courtesy of the Charleston Museum.*

Opposite: General P.G.T. Beauregard's French-made pigskin saddle was seized and sold as "confiscated goods" in Massachusetts. *Courtesy of the Ancient and Honorable Artillery Company of Massachusetts.*

Pease & Corn Bread again. Flour is $70.00…Supper if you can call it such, a cup of Malt & Corn Bread, This is no idle talk, it is either that or nothing…Maddnes [sic] *has brought ruin upon the whole country.*[142]

From late 1863 straight through to war's end, despair and privation permeated Charleston. Finally, on February 15, 1865, General Beauregard ordered his near-depleted garrison to begin their final preparations for evacuating the city. Of course, according to the standard operating procedure of the day, nothing was to be left behind that might aid the enemy. Confederate troops burned away thousands of cotton bales, along with the warehouses that held them. Railroad and machine shops were detonated, the deafening booms of which petrified most remaining townspeople into thinking enemy troops were already invading. Confederates additionally blew up ammunition dumps, destroyed their artillery, sank their gunships and set the bridge to James Island ablaze. As the *Charleston Courier* reported two days later: "With the small force at the disposal of the Fire Department, very little else could be done than to keep the surrounding buildings from igniting." Thus, it was in these final hours that an already overly desperate, tense and otherwise starving citizenry began to panic, the homegrown suffering merely amplifying a hopeless situation. Sure enough, things finally came to a head on February 18, 1865, when probably the most horrific civilian tragedy of the period occurred.[143]

At some point that morning, word spread quickly that, in their hasty departure, Confederate commissary officers had abandoned several hundred pounds of food, all piled up and unguarded inside the Northeastern Railroad depot at John and Meeting Streets. In a frenzied rush, scores of people crowded onto the rail platform, all clamoring for something to eat—and not seeming to care that several bales of cotton were still smoldering at its far end. Worse still, no one appeared to notice flames spreading from the cotton toward an adjacent room holding nearly two hundred barrels of gunpowder.[144]

"Another terrible explosion…the smoke of which darkened the sun" was how one eyewitness described it. Also standing nearby was eighteen-year-old Adolph Cramer, who wrote in his diary how he could only watch helplessly as "the women and children rushed in to get whatever they could. The depot was filled with powder and explosives and caught on fire and was blown up—causing the most pitiful sight I saw during the war. Women and children, about 250, were killed and wounded, and some were carried out by where we were in line on the streets, badly mutilated with their clothing burned off." Buildings not obliterated by the blast were soon consumed in

Siege of Charleston.

FIVE HUNDRED AND SIXTY-SEVENTH DAY.

It is evident to all that a great and important change in the affairs and government of our city is about to take place. Of the military reasons and causes which have rendered this result inevitable, it is not our purpose or desire now to speak. As journalists, however, we are called upon to restrain our feelings, and ask our citizens to suppress, as far as possible, all over excitement and disorder or confusion naturally consequent to our present and prospective condition. Let every assistance be given our worthy Mayor in his efforts to preserve order. Any citizen able and willing to aid in this duty can do so by enrolling his name in one of the Ward organizations, the lists of which will be found at the Orphan House.

Request by the *Courier* asking readers to remain calm in the face of invasion. *Courtesy of the Post and Courier.*

the ensuing fire. Within the hour, each of the separate warehouse fires set by retreating Confederate soldiers joined up with the house fires and train station conflagration like links in a chain. For the second time in four years, the city was in flames from east to west, river to river.[145]

Even in the months leading up to Charleston's military evacuation, however, there had been troubles. Venturing into the lower peninsula in December 1864, Alfred and Louis Manigault made note that, within the entire region south of Broad Street, there was "not a soul to be seen in this Godforsaken section of the City…[It] is so deserted that Thieves are going about night and day, cutting and carrying off the Copper Pumps and Lead

Northeastern Railroad depot as it appeared after a massive explosion on February 18, 1865. *Library of Congress*.

pipes of all the Cisterns." Unfortunately, the presence of roving criminals would continue to be commonplace among the shelled and burned-out city for many years to come.[146]

In the face of "northern aggression," local bandits and thieves only exacerbated the city's woes. "There has been a complete upheaval in society," wrote the *Charleston Daily News*. "It has become demoralized; from the infant in the cradle to the gray-haired man, all are more or less affected. Stealing, lynching, plundering, have become common, while human life is not respected." Of course, local readers might have more easily digested this information were it written during those first few weeks or months after the Confederate surrender. Unfortunately for them, it was still front-page material more than a year later.[147]

"Charleston A.D. 1864" map by Robert Sneden. Note the large burned area around the Northeastern Railroad depot (shown as "Wilmington Depot"). *Library of Congress.*

Newspapers statewide filled page after page with what had become an unparalleled postwar crime wave. Muggers, arsonists and especially thieves prowled the city both individually and in groups. From June 23, 1866: "Quite a brisk business was done last week…burglariously entering stores and private houses, and committing other crimes and misdemeanors too numerous to mention…we advise our citizens to put good locks on their houses and outbuildings, and to keep their shooting irons in good order." From November 20: "A party…visiting the house of a Mr. John Rogers…and demanding money…carried him, his wife, and a young lady, a short distance from the house, and three of the ruffians held them down while others ransacked the house." Also, one editor's account of the overwhelming volume of bad news constantly flooding his pressroom:

The State Bank of South Carolina's lobby, showing damage from both artillery shelling and residential looting. From *Frank Leslie's Illustrated Newspaper*, April 1, 1865. *Courtesy of the Charleston Museum.*

"Upon the floor beside us is a pile of papers…in a half hour's time we have read the particulars of a dozen robberies. Outrages upon women, violent assaults, burglaries, summary [lynch mob] executions, and murders are reported as occurring everywhere."[148]

In the end, uniformed marauders as well as homegrown criminals prospered by thinning out Charleston homes, businesses and churches. Returning residents were horrified at what little was left of their lives. Personal inventories of what was missing ran pages longer than what remained, and although most were quick to blame the enemy, who was truly responsible for these thefts might still be anyone's guess.

Family losses sadly continued for decades. A massive postwar depression, followed closely by Reconstruction, left people everywhere needing money, and selling off heirlooms seemed the only way to get it. A melancholy Williams Middleton wrote to his sister how the selling of family furniture was an upsetting venture, yet one unavoidably necessary when put against

CATALOGUE

OF

Genuine - Antique - Furniture

FROM

EMINENT FAMILIES OF SOUTH CAROLINA,

INCLUDING MANY PIECES

Formerly the Property of General Thomas Francis Marion,

OF BELLE ISLE PLANTATION.

ALSO,

A Large Collection of Choice Chippendale and Sheraton
Furniture, Cut Glass, Fenders, Andirons, Etc.,

TO BE SOLD AT AUCTION BY THE

Fifth Ave. Auction Rooms.

238 Fifth Avenue,

*WEDNESDAY, THURSDAY, FRIDAY AND
SATURDAY AFTERNOONS,*

OCTOBER 17th, 18th, 19th and 20th, AT TWO O'CLOCK
EACH DAY.

WM. B. NORMAN,

AUCTIONEER.

H. N. ATKINSON, Printer, 82 Wall Street, N. Y.

Fifth Avenue Auction Rooms catalogue from October 1894. *Courtesy of the Charleston Museum.*

his house's dire structural needs: "I have not yet lost all hope of selling for a fair price some of my unnecessary furniture, and If I can succeed in this, I shall, I think be able to close in the house; we can do without the pilastering [*sic*]…"[149]

Further capitalizing on defeated Charlestonians were brokers, dealers and pickers from Northern states, who avariciously bought up tens of thousands of cherished family belongings from cash-strapped residents. Subsequently, trainloads of valuables, most with irreplaceable provenances, left town to be speedily retailed away to the rest of the world. For example, when New York City's Fifth Avenue Auction Rooms published its 1894 autumn catalogue, the cover boasted a three-day sale dedicated exclusively to "Genuine Antique Furniture from the Eminent Families of South Carolina." By the end of the weekend, the auction had sold 184 tables and chairs, 149 porcelain tablewares, sixty-eight pairs of andirons, sixty-one sideboards and chests, forty-eight silverwares, thirty candlesticks, twenty-three pieces of crystal, thirteen mirrors, ten sofas, seven beds, six paintings and one "very rare iron door knocker over 200 years old." To be sure, in a city as depressed as Charleston, in its longer than average post-bellum downturn, cash was indeed king.[150]

VII

LOSING FAITH

An 1868 appraisal compiled by a special Episcopal Diocesan committee tasked with exploring the post–Civil War "destruction of churches" in and around Charleston stated:

> *To sum up the losses of the dioceses it appears: that ten churches have been burnt; that three have disappeared; the twenty-two Parishes are suspended; that eleven parsonages have been burnt; that every church between the Savannah River and Charleston has been injured, some stripped even of weather-boarding and flooring; that almost every minister in that region of the state has lost home and library; that along the entire seaboard, from North Carolina to Georgia, where our Church had flourished for more than a century, there are but four Parishes which maintain religious services; that not one, outside the city of Charleston, can be called a living, self-sustaining Parish; that their clergy live by fishing, farming, and mechanic arts; and that almost every church has lost its communion plate, often a massive and venerable set, the donation of an English or Colonial ancestor.*[151]

Simply stated, if South Carolina churches were not the most exploited targets, they were surely the easiest. Unguarded and often unoccupied, sanctuaries all around the Carolina Lowcountry repeatedly fell victim to militaries of both sides from both wars. Therefore, given the sheer number of holy buildings peppered all around Charleston, formal tallies, audits and estimates of their cumulative postwar losses remain, in a word, overwhelming.[152]

Federal troops loitering outside St. Michael's Church at Meeting and Broad Streets. *Library of Congress.*

Redcoat attacks on churches carried a very specific motive: retribution for past sins. By the 1770s, as far as the British government was concerned, Patriot-minded preachers had become a bit too effective in spreading their brand of influence against the Crown, and most of the region's houses of worship were rabble-rousing asylums, led by traitorous clergymen spoon-feeding radical ideas of American independence to their parishioners. For the most part, they were right. St. Philip's Church rector, Bishop Robert Smith, took regular jabs at English-driven doctrine from his elevated pulpit, while others like Presbyterian minister William Tennent III preached intensely against British governmental actions, as well as "the political establishment of the Church of England."[153]

In the 1860s, the Federal army's approach to regional churches was far less discriminatory but equally as devastating. In fact, whether or not it even considered churches as the helm of the collective insurgency was, by late 1864, an entirely moot point. Sherman was bringing his "total war" to South Carolina, laying waste to whatever fortifications, railroads, homes, churches or synagogues that just happened to be in the way. After all, just as his strategy suggested, "There were no innocent civilians" in South Carolina, nor was there anything too sacred to warrant protection from his vengeful army.[154]

More than their supposed roles as hotbeds of political dissolution, however, it was the actual church buildings that proved to be the greater asset.

Churches in general—no matter the denomination—provided remarkably useful resources for marching armies. For starters, troops could efficiently refit the spacious and open sanctuaries into quarters, hospitals, storehouses or even stables, if necessary. Secondly, it was just this sort of large structure that provided generous supplies of raw materials if (or usually when) needed. That is, it was most assuredly not an uncommon occurrence for troops to physically dismantle a church of its siding, pews, lead sashes, upholstery or even its bells and subsequently reprocess these materials into stretchers, bandages, bullets or, at the very least, firewood. Damage of this type made early colonial churches like St. George's in Dorchester or St. Paul's and St. James's of Goose Creek completely uninhabitable by 1782. What was left of St. John's in Colleton County, in fact, was woefully described in 1789 as having "not a door, window shutter or pew to be seen, a large part of the floor missing, the pavement of the isles in many places destroyed, and in short no one part but indicated the necessity of some repairs."[155]

In town, Brits at the present-day Unitarian Church seriously damaged the interior when they employed the sanctuary as both barracks and a stable for their cavalry horses—scars of which were still apparent in 1858, when Reverend Samuel Gillman mentioned them during a sermon. Some miles away and decades later, two separate Presbyterian churches fell victim to Yankee axes. The first was at Stoney Creek, where soldiers stripped wooden siding and dismantled pews in order to build a bridge over the Pocotaligo River, and the second was east of the Cooper River, where bluecoats cut out every last mahogany pew in Mount Pleasant Presbyterian's sanctuary, renovating it into a makeshift hospital for their own sick and wounded. Eventually unable to refit them into bunks, the soldiers deemed the substantial pews "suitable only for burning" and proceeded then to chop rough, bed-beam support niches in the interior columns. Of course, repurposed sanctuaries worked just as well for one side as the other. The *Charleston Daily Courier*, for instance, reported on August 11, 1863, how Mount Pleasant's "Methodist Church was cheerfully given up" as a hospital to treat Confederate wounded from Battery Wagner.[156]

Thus, it became painfully obvious to commanders that leaving a church intact naturally risked benefitting the opposition, especially if fighting had not yet ended at the time of its seizure. Sadly, therefore, once it was time to move on, most enemy occupiers ignominiously burned down these churches that had hitherto served them, ensuring that their adversaries could not take similar advantage. Troops burned Mount Pleasant's Christ Church in 1782 and yet again in 1865, but not before taking advantage of its amenities. The Twenty-

Above: One of Mount Pleasant Presbyterian's several sanctuary support columns cut into by Union troops. *Courtesy of Mount Pleasant Presbyterian Church.*

Opposite: Christ Church in Mount Pleasant. *Library of Congress.*

first Massachusetts Colored Regiment camped all around the church grounds, stabled their horses in the sanctuary and burned the pews for firewood.[157]

Enemy arson consumed plenty of other small parish houses as well, including St. Stephens's, St. Mark's, St. John's Berkeley and Prince George's, just to name a scant few. It is important to note, however, that it was not always the invaders' fault, particularly when keeping in mind the great conflagration of 1861. That particular fire alone completely consumed five downtown churches, not the least of which were the esteemed Circular Church on Meeting Street, and the Cathedral of St. John and St. Finbar on

Broad. An additional, albeit unfortunate, Episcopal committee report from 1868 mentioned that its "Church on James Island was accidentally destroyed during the siege of Charleston…Some of our troops, amusing themselves in rabbit hunting, set fire to the grass in an old field. The fire communicated with the church and destroyed it."[158]

Obviously, for a church to actually survive either one—or miraculously both—of Charleston's wars without some degree of theft or damage was remarkable to say the least. However, even for those that might have survived structurally, most were robbed of assorted, left-behind possessions. Perhaps

Principal Church watercolor depicting St. Michael's Church by A. Meyer, circa 1860. *Library of Congress.*

only through divine intervention did St. Michael's Church, at the corner of Meeting and Broad Streets, avoid serious damage despite coming under heavy artillery fire first in 1780 and again for more than a year and a half between 1863 and 1865.

During the British siege, cannonballs fired from naval vessels and land batteries on James Island barely missed St. Michael's. One particular shot struck the William Pitt statue, which at the time stood a mere forty-five feet or so from the front door. Decades later, Union artillerymen used St. Michael's venerable steeple as a sighting point, this time with new large-bore and long-range guns on Morris Island. Still, the church withstood.

Unsurprisingly, though, it was the hands of the enemy and not its weaponry that diminished St. Michael's. In one of the more direct and obvious exploits of British thievery, redcoats removed the large and extremely heavy set of eight bells (each cast specifically for the church in 1764) from the steeple, set them aboard a vessel and shipped all eight "for sale in England." Thankfully, a kind-hearted—and clearly well-to-do—British merchant listed only as "Mr. Ryhineu" purchased all eight and returned them to Charleston.[159]

St. Michael's bells were removed once again in 1863, this time by church officials unwilling to make the same mistake as their predecessors. Once the Federal bombardment commenced, the bells, organ, silver and assorted other items were all removed "to a place of safety"—or so it was thought. The organ, remarkably, returned unscathed, but as the diocese reported in 1868, the silver was lost and "its chime bells, one of the best in the country, was not so fortunate. They were sent to Columbia, and placed in a shed in the State House yard. The Federal soldiers set fire to the shed and the heat cracked and destroyed the bells." One resident returning to town at war's end sorrowfully described their loss:

> *Their absence on our return to the city, filled us with more melancholy emotions than almost any connected with this war. From our boyhood we had been familiar with their tones…When finding ourselves within the sound of their chimes, the Bells of St. Michael gave forth no sound. Our first question would have been, who has done this, if we had not recollected the war had visited our venerable city. The ravage of fields, the devastation of cities, the destruction of records, the mutilation of monuments, are visitations of sufficient severity; but in the mere wantonness of a spirit of mischief, and from the sole pleasure of destroying, to aim at the destruction of a spire…like St. Michael's would be beyond belief, if the fact were not so recent as to be without denial.[160]*

Occasionally, besides exploiting churches for materials and shelter, clever-thinking officers found unexpected uses for empty sanctuaries and even their surrounding grounds. Such was the case of Prince William's Parish Church near Beaufort. Commonly referred to today as Sheldon, its ruins still provide a surreal reminder of the Patriot struggle.

In 1745, at the request of Lieutenant Governor William Bull, the Commons House of Assembly established Prince William's Parish. The site chosen for the church was adjacent to Bull's own Sheldon Plantation. Completed by 1754, Bull spared little expense on the "Church at Sheldon," which some described as more of a Roman temple than a local house of worship.

An elegant place of public worship, the resort and pride of the wealthy Episcopalians in that part of the district. It was a bond of union and of good fellowship among the neighbors...Here they met, kneeled together at the same altar, suspending all feelings of political animosity and personal enmity...This church was the chief object of their admiration, in which all partook with equal warmth.[161]

That was, at least, until Tory and parish native Major Andrew Deveaux Jr. ordered it burned in 1779. What Deveaux would later casually describe as a "frolicsome episode" was in reality a cavalcade of rapine and mayhem. Advancing northward from the Coosawhatchie River, Deveaux's militia and some accompanying British regulars entered Prince William's Parish and occupied its village of McPhersonville. From there, the hunt was on. Of furniture, silver and clothing, not a piece went unmolested, according to the *South Carolina Gazette*. Another source recorded sexual assaults on local women, the slaughter of livestock and the roundup of some four thousand slaves, who were subsequently "shipped to the West Indies and sold." By the time Deveaux and his men turned toward Sheldon Church, nearly all of McPhersonville lay in smoldering embers.[162]

His conquest aside, Deveaux still had at least two problems that needed addressing. The first involved a long-standing rumor that William Bull's brother Stephen was secreting gunpowder at Sheldon Church and had been since 1775, when an English ship carrying sixteen thousand pounds of it was captured at Tybee Island. The second and perhaps more worrisome issue concerned a small but measurable undercurrent of unrest among his own men. Their confidence shaken after an unexpected defeat at Port Royal some weeks prior, murmurings and general anxieties over just who was actually going to win the war had begun surfacing.[163]

Ruins of Sheldon Church as they appear today. Burned during the Revolution, the church was rebuilt in 1826 but seriously damaged again by Union forces during their 1865 assault on McPhersonville. *Author's photo.*

Fortunately, Deveaux found a common thread linking his two conundrums and smartly seized an opportunity to kill two birds with one stone. "Determined," as he put it, "to commit [the troops] by some glaring act of hostility" and probably believing that burning down a holy place would somehow convince his men of King George's infallibility, Deveaux wasted little time in setting his Tory torchbearers on the church. Besides, he thought, even if the act failed to shore up his men's royalist ideals, would it not at least deprive the rebels of their gunpowder stash? Apparently not.[164]

As thorough as the redcoats were in obliterating Sheldon Church, it is interesting to note that General Francis Marion was still encamped there at the end of the year and, furthermore, apparently sitting atop what must have been a small mountain of gunpowder. In fact, writing from Sheldon two days before Christmas 1779, Marion sent a short letter to an unnamed recipient and ordered him to "immediately as possible send to camp as much cartridge paper as will make Eighty thousand Cartridges." Indubitably, it appears that Deveaux and his men missed a spot, if not several, focusing too much on Sheldon's building and not enough on its graveyard. Like many wealthier churches around Charleston, Sheldon was not without its share of low-lying, box tombs (sometimes called box graves or chest tombs), a common grave-marker form appearing throughout the colonies by the mid-eighteenth century. The name derives from its construction: a four-sided rectangular foundation of brick or stone built above ground, outlining the decedent's burial plot and topped and covered with an engraved slab of slate or marble. It stands to reason, then, just as some have speculated over the years, that Marion took full advantage of these large, sturdy and, more importantly, enclosed grave markers and, betting on the Brits' usual unwillingness to desecrate graves, used Sheldon's box tombs as gunpowder repositories.[165]

When it came to graveyards and cemeteries, redcoats for the most part, mercifully, avoided disturbing them. If only the same could be said of the Union soldiers. Their overwhelming numbers, unleashed in the Lowcountry by 1865, deemed nothing sacred. Around Charleston, holy ground was no more protected than any other place. One account taken by clergymen of the Episcopal diocese noted, "The repositories of the dead were, in several places opened, and the grave itself searched for hidden treasure." Unbridled burglarizing was equally horrifying at St. Andrew's, just southeast of Drayton Hall. "The demon of civil war was let loose in this Parish," read one report. "Fire and sword were not enough. Family vaults were rifled, and the coffins of the dead forced open in pursuit of plunder." The same held true for estates. Writing from nearby Middleton Place, Williams Middleton mournfully reflected how both former servants and Union men "sufficiently wreaked upon me…the scattering of the remains of my forefathers from the tomb…and the carrying off of the contents of two of the coffins."[166]

Mercifully, many clerics and congregants from both the eighteenth and nineteenth centuries foresaw the dangers concomitant to enemy invasion and took as many appropriate measures as could be afforded. In 1782, for example, members of Christ Church somehow removed its sacred silver from the sanctuary before retreating bands of redcoats could confiscate it—something they would have to do all over again in the mid-1860s. Still, not all efforts met with equal success. "I took with me the sacramental vessels of the church, in a large black box," wrote Reverend Anthony Toomer Porter of Charleston's Church of the Holy Communion. "I had placed a box containing books and clothing, sermons and valuable papers, in charge of a friend…but in confusion he lost the box. The sermons, clothing, and valuable papers, I never heard from again. I wonder if General Sherman's men read the sermons! They were some of my best, and I would like to get hold of some of them myself!" Regrettably, when analyzing rectory notes, clerical journals and personal letters, Reverend Porter's experiences were by no means unique.[167]

Middleton Family tomb at Middleton Place. *Library of Congress.*

As noted earlier, it is hardly surprising that Bishop Robert Smith of St. Philip's Church endured repeated harassments for most of 1779. After all, he himself had "shouldered his musket" in defense of Fort Sullivan, and since that day in 1776, the good bishop had become fiercely protective of Carolinian rights. Commissioned as chaplain general in the Southern

Silver chalice (marked by Boston silversmith John Edwards circa 1705) belonging to Christ Church in Mount Pleasant. *Courtesy of Christ Church, Mount Pleasant; photo by Keith Leonard.*

Department of the Continental army, he was certainly not content to handle just the spiritual side of soldiering, nor was he one to back away from his own words. He preached against all forms of British influence; his eloquent orations persuaded many of those previously undecided on independence to shift their loyalty to the Patriot cause. "The good Christian cannot be an unconcerned spectator of any great degree of wickedness," he said during one particular sermon, "even while he himself stands free from the detection of it."[168]

Over the course of the war, Smith's convictions and very public derisions of the Crown did not go unnoticed—or ultimately unpunished—by his British adversaries, and not long after Charleston capitulated, he was made an example to the rest of his rebellion-minded flock. By late spring of 1780, the Brits had placed Smith's name near the top of a long list of persons marked for property confiscation. After its seizure, his Brabant Plantation was in the possession of General Charles Cornwallis, who took up residence in the main house, employing it as his headquarters and subsequently dispersing most of its furnishings to his subordinates:

> *His household furniture, consisting of bedsteads, feather beds, mattrasses [sic], mahogany dining, sideboard, breakfast, tea, dressing, and night tables, wash-stands, chairs, dressing glasses, small pier, and a remarkable octagon inlaid frame looking-glass; blue and white table china, glass ware, fire dogs, shovels and tongs, kitchen furniture of all Sorts, &c., &c., was made use of or lent out...few articles have been recovered.*[169]

Fortunately, five extraordinarily important pieces of silver dating to 1729—two flagons, an alms basin, a patent and chalice—went unmolested during Cornwallis's stay. However, that is not the same as saying that this particularly stunning communion service was overlooked. In the days leading up to Charleston's capture, Smith had personally secured much of his church's sacramental material, and not about to leave the valuable communion service unprotected—each piece a gift to the congregation of St. Philips from King George II and bearing detailed engravings of his royal coat-of-arms—Smith took the service home to Brabant. There, together with an overseer named Mauder, they buried it.[170]

Now, with each piece clearly marked for their former monarch, British troops still considered the silver to be royal property, and they wanted it back. Soldiers searched St. Philip's but found nothing, leaving them to assume that perhaps Smith or someone else at Brabant knew of its location.

The King's silver of St. Philip's Church (marked by London silversmiths Joseph Allen and Mordecai Fox in 1729) buried by Bishop Robert Smith at Brabant Plantation. *Courtesy of St. Philip's Church; photo by Keith Leonard.*

Thus, determined to reclaim the "King's silver," the redcoats took out their frustrations on Mauder.[171]

Preparing a noose, officers at Brabant wasted little time in ordering Mauder's torture, resurrecting an old strangulation method from their medieval forebears: hanging the poor man from a tree but not dropping him so fast as to snap his neck. Mauder was suspended three separate times, each one bringing him ever closer to death. Amazingly, though, he never gave up the whereabouts of the silver, later declaring that "the sacredness of the Communion vessels" gave him the strength to keep his secret. Because of this remarkable feat, the King's silver remains safely in the church's possession to this day.[172]

Now, even if churches managed to avoid looting, stripping or arson and remained structurally intact, they still faced massive challenges, specifically in regards to their congregations—or lack thereof. As officials at St. Andrew's Parish recorded in 1865:

> *This venerable church built in 1706, survives—but in the midst of a desert. Every residence but one, on the west bank of the Ashley River, was*

burnt simultaneously with the evacuation of Charleston, by the besieging forces from James Island. Many of these were historical homes in South Carolina; the abodes of refinement and hospitality for more than a century past. The residence of the Rector was embowered in one of the most beautiful gardens which nature and art can create—more than two hundred varieties of camellia, combined with stately avenues of magnolia, to delight the eye even of European visitors. But not a vestige remains, save the ruins of his ancestral home.[173]

Of the few parish houses spared the redcoats' torch between 1780 and 1782, most had, through lack of occupancy and maintenance, deteriorated to a state of ruin. Vestry notes from St. John's in Colleton County, for example, describe what was left of the place in 1789 as "in a most deplorable situation...not a door, window, shutter, or pew to be seen, a large part of the floor missing." No less spared were the larger downtown churches, most of them abandoned by their once vibrant congregations. St. Philip's next-door neighbor, the French Huguenot Church, besides having its silver stolen from a hiding place in Cheraw, had nary a worshiper left in 1865. A pastor there noted, "There were left very few persons of means whose devotion and liberality maintained the church, but these are all dead; other adherents have removed from the city, and the congregation has at last become so small that it cannot sustain the church."[174]

A few blocks farther south, elders at First (Scots) Presbyterian Church were taking stock of their sanctuary and its sacramental furnishings at the end of the Civil War. Miraculously, their stately communion wares remained safely hidden away in Camden and would soon be on their way back to the church. Whatever became of all the communion tokens, on the other hand, was anyone's guess.

Continuing an old, heralded Scottish practice from the 1500s, both First (Scots) and Second Presbyterian churches in Charleston continued to incorporate communion tokens in their services right up until the outbreak of war in 1861. As the name suggests, these quarter-sized pieces provided a ticket of sorts to those wishing to partake in the sacrament, and getting one was not always an easy task. In fact, congregants had to interview for the privilege. In the days leading up to a communion service, those seeking a "place at the table" met with elders, who, in turn, examined "his or her knowledge of the faith." Those who passed, of course, received a token that they would turn in the following Sunday and thus receive the sacrament. Those who failed...well, better luck next time.[175]

Of interest about First (Scots), however, was its predominant use of silver communion tokens. These were a flashy upgrade, to be sure, and

Silver communion token (obverse and reverse) from First (Scots) Presbyterian Church. *Courtesy of First (Scots) Presbyterian Church; photo by Keith Leonard.*

a more expensive way of "honoring thy God," as opposed to the more typical examples of copper, tin, lead or pewter commonly found in most other Presbyterian churches around Europe and America. Disappointingly, though, just like so many other local houses of worship, indiscriminate Union shelling of the city forced the removal of portable church property. But instead of piling everything into a single trunk and shipping it off, the elders of First (Scots) wisely separated their valuables and evacuated them to several inland destinations. Unlike the things sent to Camden, though, enemy troops discovered what appears to have been the entire collection of approximately three hundred silver and five hundred supplemental pewter tokens, which had been crated and carted off to Columbia. Since then, only five have actually been returned.[176]

Refreshingly, perhaps because of their uniqueness and obvious markings around the rims ("The Presbyterian Church of Charleston, S.C. 1800"), the silver tokens of First (Scots) are, for the most part, easy to spot. Because of this, additional tokens have come to light. In 1962, for example, Donald I. Blue of Ohio sent a silver token back to the congregation. His enclosed note, while stopping short of revealing just how he acquired it, at least offered his genuine condolences: "To First (Scots) Presbyterian Church, Charleston, S.C., 1862–1962. After 100 years sojourn in the North. May the return of this Communion Token to the South help cement the ties of brotherly love between us." Moreover, in the summer of 1865, an anonymous Yankee infantryman handed over a rather heavily tarnished token to a North Carolina family in exchange for some food. It took some sixty years, but the family eventually turned the piece over to Reverend Dr. Alexander Sprunt, who subsequently placed it in the protection of the Presbyterian Historical Foundation in Montreat, North Carolina, where it remains.[177]

LOST AND FOUND

Four years to the day after surrendering Fort Sumter to the Confederacy—and mere hours before President Lincoln would be assassinated in Washington—Union general Robert Anderson was back to reclaim it for the United States, by re-raising the same flag he had been forced to remove back on April 14, 1861. Although a bouquet of roses was sewn to it for the event, after Anderson's flag whipped in the wind for a spell, the flowers broke free and fell to the ground. Only after the ceremony's conclusion was the bouquet casually picked up by one of Sherman's majors in attendance, Dr. Thomas J. Saunders, who, thinking it a nice memento, kept it.[178]

Returning to his Iowa home, Saunders pressed the bouquet and framed it. After his death, his son handed over the now brown-and-lifeless floral arrangement to a family friend, who, in 1953, passed it off again to an anonymous associate. Although its actual travels cannot be determined, the bouquet apparently continued to change hands around Iowa over the next twenty years. Finally, in 1973, someone came to recognize the bouquet's Charleston heritage and sent it back.[179]

Predictably, official postwar audits of missing goods were painfully slow to materialize, and governing agents usually ignored them even when they did. It is in this regard, then, that church minutes, estate inventories, newspaper reports and especially family letters become all-important ingredients in attempting to rediscover Charleston's lost or so-called liberated treasures. Refreshingly—although uncommonly—recoveries of

Flag-raising ceremony at Fort Sumter, April 14, 1865. *Library of Congress.*

artifacts once believed long lost certainly have occurred from time to time. It is these reclamations that still provide uplifting examples of survival amid turmoil.

Charlestonians struggled after the wars to reclaim at least some semblance of the life they had enjoyed beforehand. Some, through due diligence and luck, succeeded. Many others did not. Indeed, South Carolinians had gained a thorough understanding of the ways of warfare by the 1780s, having been quite thoroughly stripped of their properties. Fed up in those final days of the British evacuation, state officials worked to protect citizens from straggling redcoat marauders, going so far as to appoint Benjamin Guerard and Edward Rutledge as commissioners of a Privy Council. Yet in negotiating as best they could with British officers to ensure a peaceful departure from Charleston, the council's endeavors proved fruitless, and illicit plundering of local civilians continued for months.[180]

Pressed bouquet of roses from Fort Sumter's April 14, 1865 flag-raising ceremony framed by Thomas J. Saunders and kept in his Iowa home. *Courtesy of the Charleston Museum.*

Concession demands even after the redcoats were gone fared no better. Henry Laurens, who by serving as a peace commissioner in 1782 actually had a realistic chance at recompense, failed miserably in his arguments that the British government be held accountable for military thievery. He pushed for stipulations in both the preliminary and final drafts of the

Treaty of Paris that would have required any and all property stolen by the British army to be paid for by Parliament, but none was included. What had to have been even more galling to him, royal administrators actually confirmed that £2,800 in stolen goods from his very estates was "lying in the British treasury" but would remain "unpaid lest its payment should encourage similar claims."[181]

Though instrumental in gaining independence for his country—and getting locked in the Tower of London because of it—Laurens seethed and brooded over the damage done to nonmilitary targets in and around Charleston during its British occupation, his sadness clear in a 1782 letter to William Manning:

> *The Minds of the People are sore & many of their Bodies too from Opression* [sic] *and Grievances…These Truths will be more fully and clearly manifested in a cooler hour, and Britania* [sic] *will then blush for shame of her elders sons, perhaps put her hand to her Pocket and pay all Damages. Tears in these melancholy Moments are too ready in my eye, this subject has led me into Reflections which have drawn forth a flood; looking at the Land smoaking* [sic] *from the Embers of Towns and Cities, echoing the shrieks of ravished Virgins, crimsoned with the blood of brave Defenders, and of many an Innocent Infant massacred by the hands of Britain's ruthless allies, I cannot refrain from tears.*[182]

Still, not all was lost. Although it would take many years and unyielding conviction, Charlestonians were then, as now, a tough bunch and certainly not the types to let missing things stay that way—at least not forever.

Martha Sullivan, for one, never questioned why her husband could never let go of the old legend of Strawberry Chapel's communion silver. Holding a gas lantern for him night after night, while he probed the dirt subfloor beneath Comingtee Plantation's rice mill, had slowly evolved from a once-whimsical scavenger hunt to a half-baked holy quest.

Named for a nearby bluff on the Cooper River's east side, Strawberry Chapel was commissioned by a 1720s act of assembly, with an initial plan for it to serve as the central meeting and worship house for the 1707 township of Childsbury. Though Childsbury withered, the chapel survived and thrived. As its congregation expanded, so too did its assets, eventually acquiring from its parent parish house a stunning coin-silver patent and chalice marked by Charleston "goldsmith" Miles Brewton, a remarkable artisan and among the earliest metalworkers in the colony.[183]

Strawberry Chapel. *Library of Congress.*

Even though Strawberry Chapel and its silver miraculously survived the Brits and their plundering protocols of the early 1780s, the events of 1865 would be a slightly different story.

By late February 1865, Keating Ball already knew the fates of most Ashley River plantations and outlying parish houses: they were in ashes. Thus, it was only a matter of time—hours perhaps—before troops would be streaming up the Cooper River toward Keating's generations-old family home, Comingtee Plantation, named for the area's first English settler, John Coming, and a geographical T-shaped fork formed by two branches of the river. The Ball family had been instrumental in sustaining Strawberry Chapel since its establishment, worshiping there regularly and serving on the vestry generation after generation. Certainly not one to abandon this family tradition, Keating had served as chairman of the vestry before the war and near its end was still acting as Strawberry's warden—an unenviable position in light of the current disorder that surrounded him.[184]

Keating had already traveled the two-mile stretch to Strawberry earlier in the day to retrieve the church's five-piece communion service—which included the two Brewton-made pieces and the mahogany chest that held them. He stored them in his closet, while a few slaves "helped him bury the family silver and hide the portraits…" His own belongings secured, Keating moved on to protecting the Strawberry items, turning to his most trusted servant, a slave named "Friday," to help hide its silver.

By nightfall, with Charleston, its periphery and waterways becoming more and more crowded with Federal troops, the pair could delay no longer. Friday, with Keating following closely, carried the chest from Comingtee's main house over to its rice mill, removed some floorboards and lowered himself into a waist-deep pit. There, working in near-total darkness with only a single lantern between them, Friday buried Strawberry Chapel's most prized possessions in the dirt, while Keating remained above ground making sure no one—no one—witnessed the act.[185]

Mercifully, Yankee troops spared the torch at both Comingtee and Strawberry Chapel, although Keating was never sure exactly why. Indeed several soldiers had come calling in the days following his and Friday's covert operation, but thanks in large part to Keating's hospitality, having "so gentle yet firm a courtesy…the officer in command not only restrained his men but gave a paper of protection." Finally, after a few tense weeks and months, things settled down just enough to consider a renewal of Sunday services at Strawberry, and of everyone on the vestry, none was more eager than Keating to retrieve the silver.

> But…when they returned to the mill to recover the buried chest, they could not find it, Digging at the spot which Friday was sure was the right one, they turned up only black soil. Keating Ball—who hadn't actually gone under the mill—realized that he couldn't be sure of the exact spot. As for Friday, his mind had been in a turmoil that night. Sure that a further search would reveal the chest, they had probed and dug everywhere, covering, as they thought, practically the whole of the extensive area under the mill. Though they returned again and again to the task they found nothing.[186]

Over the next dozen years or so, Keating and a few other Ball family members tried again and again to find Strawberry Chapel's lost silver but eventually gave up, concluding that someone had seen the twosome's exploits that night and either stole it or "betrayed it to the Federal raiders." When Keating Ball died in 1891, the real story of what had actually happened to Strawberry Chapel's communion silver appeared to go with him. Truly his death was a critical one insofar as it all but erased whatever factual evidence or intricate knowledge had existed up until then of the silver's whereabouts. Over the course of time, its history morphed into hazy legend.[187]

Within a half century of Keating's death, in fact, Comingtee and a few other neighboring plantations had all been converted into a collective hunting preserve, with Grover Sullivan working as the property superintendent. In January 1946, however, his somewhat predictable routine was altered by an interesting phone call informing him that Mrs. Charlotte Ball, daughter to one of Keating's cousins, would be stopping by to explore some old story of buried treasure that her father had once insisted was true. Of course, both Grover and his wife, Martha, knew the legend, having heard countless retellings of it since moving onto the property, and knowing Charlotte to be a member of Comingtee's long-heralded Ball family, they were happy to oblige her curiosity.[188]

What neither of the Sullivans knew, however, was who and, more importantly, what Charlotte was bringing with her. Apparently, with World War II won and done, geological, archaeological and historical institutions had taken to buying up surplus metal detectors, and this had given Charlotte an idea. At her urging, a close friend with ties to New York's Fort Ticonderoga made some calls, ultimately convincing the site's general manager, Milo King, to bring his newly acquired device down to Charleston and hopefully settle once and for all the matter of Strawberry's lost silver.[189]

Following Charlotte's version of the tale and with metal detector at the ready, Milo, Charlotte, Martha, Grover and a few others descended on Comingtee. The group was soon creeping from the main house to the rice mill and then down into the depths of the crawlspace. Martha later recalled the day's less-than-exciting events: "There must have been I don't know how many nails and old pieces of metal and all under there," and every last one set the detector off in a frenzy of beeps and chirps. For hours the work continued, and by day's end, the group's struggles had produced only a few handfuls of nails, some broken milling parts and a rusted-out iron sheet. A visibly disappointed Charlotte raised herself from below ground and departed Comingtee empty-handed. Milo King left with the metal detector the next morning.[190]

For them, the search was over, but for whatever reason, Grover and Martha remained unsatisfied by the luckless escapade beneath Comingtee's rice mill. After a sleepless night or two, both decided they would continue the search and perhaps at last remedy Keating Ball's misfortune. Though Grover's job kept him busy during the day, he and Martha returned to the rice mill night after hapless night for almost a week. Finally, on what Grover

Strawberry Chapel's silver service buried in 1865 and recovered in 1946 from beneath the rice mill at Comingtee Plantation. *Courtesy of the Vestry of Strawberry Chapel; photo by Keith Leonard.*

said would be their last night of digging and searching, Martha watched her husband find Strawberry Chapel's silver.

> *It was as black down there in the daytime as it was at night…and we'd go down there at night with a lantern and look for it after the day's work was over. After about three or four nights, my husband said, "Look at this—there's something here." He had a long rod and he mashed down in there and heard it hit metal. The box that it was in was practically deteriorated by that time, but we got it out. Each piece had an inscription on it…The church was still active so it belonged to them.*[191]

A ruin today, the rice mill at Comingtee Plantation for more than eighty-one years sat atop a historical treasure that very easily could have become one of South Carolina's greatest losses. Obviously, the Sullivans' tenacity, fortitude and patience were instrumental in solving the mystery left behind by Keating Ball, but the sheer significance of the find is remarkable on multiple levels. First, the near-unbelievable rediscovery of Strawberry Chapel's silver, in one fell swoop, brought back two marked pieces from Miles Brewton, a key figure in Charleston's early artisan class. Secondly, the patent and chalice now join his two other surviving chalices as the four earliest examples of southern-made silver in existence, a collection vital to the study of American decorative arts.

Now, although the case of Strawberry Chapel's unearthed silver remains today a testament to a conscientious and determined endeavor to reclaim a wartime loss, there are certainly other accounts where plain, old blind luck stepped in. Thankfully, as the *Charleston Daily News* reported in its December 13, 1866 edition, there were other miracles: an anonymous "old hunter recently found $7,000 in gold and silver buried in a keg"—a stash no doubt lost during the Union occupation.

Indeed, many members of Charleston's Manigault family returned to their homes to recoup and rebuild, but as for Charlotte Morris Manigault, she was through. With their house robbed and gutted completely by enemy troops, she and her husband, Henry Heyward Manigault, decided to simply abandon the States entirely and make Europe their new and permanent home. Before their transatlantic exodus, however, the couple first traveled to New York to make proper banking preparations, and it was there that Charlotte won her own personal victory against the North.[192]

Although in New York only briefly, Charlotte still made time for Sunday service at Grace Church on Broadway, since the rector, Dr. Henry C. Potter, was an acquaintance of her brother Charles. Entering the sanctuary and choosing what she thought was a "convenient pew," she was soon startled by an older couple gesturing for her to move from what were their customary seats. As the service was already underway but moreover because she was unwilling to relent to yet another northerner, Charlotte refused their request, leaving the discourteous strangers no choice but to accept defeat and sit beside her.[193]

It was only after the service ended that the real atonement began. Before her new neighbors could leave the pew, Charlotte stopped the scowling woman, adamantly requesting that she "accompany her to the Vestry Room," where she had "an important statement to make to her in the presence of the Rector." Resentful but curious, the woman followed Charlotte out of the sanctuary, whereupon they were able to catch up with Dr. Potter, who, ever the patient man of the cloth, granted the two angry women an audience. In a family letter, Charlotte described how she began the meeting, saying, "Dr. Potter, you know my brother, Captain (Charles) Morris of the United States Navy. My brother bought me a beautiful India shawl from one of his voyages, which I prize highly as a gift from him, and that shawl was stolen from my house during the War, and this lady is wearing it…It has my monogram embroidered in the corner." Amazingly still not finished, Charlotte continued, "That bracelet you have on was given me by my father when I was married. It has a hidden spring by pressing which, my father's miniature will appear." Potter inspected both the shawl and the bracelet without hesitation and quickly confirmed Charlotte's monogram at the shawl's corner and her father's miniature portrait hidden within the bracelet's locket. At Potter's request, the wearer returned the items to their rightful owner, never divulging how, when or, more importantly, from whom she had received them.[194]

Besides Charlotte Manigault's good fortune, further examples of Charlestonians' divine luck, while certainly unusual, were refreshingly imitable. An equally fascinating account of a chance run-in between Peter C. Gaillard and a pair of family portraits is most certainly worthy of mention.

Left with only a mirror and sewing table intact after Union soldiers pillaged and burned their Edisto home, Thomas and Dorothea Black spent years rebounding from the trampled wreck the war had left them with. Though able to replace much of what they had lost, the theft of two cherished portraits illustrating Dorothea's uncle and aunt, Francis and Anne deLiesseline, had left a void in the family history. With the paintings gone, the deLiesselines' only likenesses had been expunged—or so it seemed.[195]

Twenty years later, in 1886, Peter C. Gaillard—former mayor, gallant Confederate veteran and friend of the Blacks' daughter, Martha L.E. "Mattie" Kirk—was in Boston and, in all probability, less than pleased to be there. As both a soldier and politician, the former colonel had endured plenty of run-ins with his former northern adversaries over the previous decades. On this occasion, he was on the home turf of a former nemesis, General Benjamin "Beast" Butler, a man with whom he and his Twenty-seventh South Carolina Infantry had faced off against and beaten at Cold Harbor. The "Beast," nevertheless, was still very much alive and, moreover, a favorite subject of southern newspapers. It seemed, according to the *Charleston Daily News* anyway, that Butler's home in Lowell was a "receptacle of stolen goods," filled with "magnificent pictures…plundered from one of the elegant mansions of New Orleans." Fortunately, Butler had never been in Charleston during the war, so whatever looted goods might or might not have been decorating his house were unlikely to be of local origin. Still, the numerous news reports—all of which Gaillard would have read—had to have been on his mind as he walked the Boston streets.[196]

Portrait of Anne deLiesseline taken from Edisto Island in 1865, purchased in Boston by Peter C. Gaillard and returned to the family. *Private collection; photo by Sean Money.*

Perhaps because of this, he was quick to notice Anne and Francis deLiesselines' portraits, seemingly peering back at him from behind a storefront window. For Gaillard, there was no mistaking his fellow congregants from the French Huguenot Church in the years before the war. More than that, Francis deLiesseline was not exactly an unknown Charleston figure, having served as county sheriff in the 1820s. So, in what some might consider his last act of Confederate gallantry, Gaillard liberated the stolen portraits from the antiques store—by purchasing them honestly—and returned them to Mattie later that summer. In her September 24, 1886 letter to Gaillard, Mattie thanked him profusely for "restoring the treasured relics to their proper representatives…to whom are the lawful custodians." Both portraits remain in the family.[197]

Perhaps lucky is too light a word to describe the chance circumstances of Charlotte Manigault and Peter Gaillard, yet as any antique dealer, collector or curator will attest, happenstance is an important component in rescuing heirlooms from the unknown. Unfortunately, of course, the aforementioned examples are merely a scarce few happy endings in an otherwise black hole of what-went-where.

Henrietta Aiken Rhett, for instance, in writing to Judge Charles H. Simonton in December 1866, pleaded for his assistance in carrying out "a claim against the United States Government for silverware taken by Sherman's troops…" All attempts failed, and Rhett died in her Elizabeth Street home (now Charleston's Aiken-Rhett House Museum) having never seen her silver again.[198]

Of all that Charles Manigault lamented losing in 1865, he appeared particularly distraught at the theft of his "most rare and valuable…Elephant coin of Carolina 1694." Describing how "this coin had been preserved in our family for several generations…One side the coin has upon it an Elephant, and on the reverse it bears the inscription 'God preserve Carolina and the Lords proprietors.'" Charles would painfully find out his coin's fate barely two years later. On May 3, 1867, a New York newspaper printed a listing of various auctioned-off lots, among which was a "Carolina elephant piece of 1694," sold for a measly $26.50. As Louis Manigault wrote woefully, "Most probably this was our coin," now lost amongst the anonymous public.[199]

As previously mentioned, while Williams Middleton had been unable to recover his water buffalo, he was at least able to learn where they ended up. His luck would be better—but only slightly so—in regards to other plundered possessions. About a week before Yankee troops showed up on the doorstep of Middleton Place, Williams had removed as much as practicable from his home, although there was no possible way to save it all. Furniture, paintings and somewhere between eight thousand and ten thousand bound volumes remained behind, wide open to whatever abuses the Feds could dream up and dish out.

Arriving on February 23, 1865, Dr. Henry Marcy, a Union army medical director, took advantage. "The House was strewed with articles and all

Louis Manigault's sketches (obverse and reverse) of his father's stolen and sold "elephant coin." *Private collection; photo by Sean Money.*

At a sale of coins in New York on Friday evening, a silver dollar, coined 1764, brought $42 50; a half-dime dated 1794, was purchased for $9, and a cent dated 1799, sold for $20. An "Edwards counterfeit" half cent of 1796 brought $5 25, and a Carolina elephant piece of 1694 was sold for $26 50. 3 May 1867

New York newspaper clipping reporting the sale of what was likely Charles Manigault's coin. *Private collection; photo by Sean Money.*

about the grounds things were scattered," he wrote. "There were many paintings yet in the house—hundreds of frames. I selected a few small ones." Also unwilling to let so many books go to waste, Marcy returned some months later to find "a quantity of books laying about all over the grounds, some hidden in the woods…much injured by dampness and mould [*sic*] but in other aspects much as I left them in February." Having already taken approximately twenty paintings, Marcy loaded up all the books his wagon could carry, later admitting that despite the enormous haul, "we left a boatload."[200]

Unfortunately for Dr. Marcy, concealing such a large treasure-trove was impossible, and when Williams eventually heard an eyewitness account of the doctor's shenanigans, he was unsurprisingly livid. He wrote to his sister, Eliza, on September 16, 1866: "I have ascertained that a certain Dr. Marcy has in his possession several of my most valuable & interesting pictures & other objects of more or less value." Also corresponding with his brother, Edward, a former Union navy captain then living in New York, Williams made known his frustrations and asked his sibling to immediately investigate the possibility of getting his paintings back. Wholly embarrassed that his blue-uniformed colleagues had partaken in such grand thievery and incensed that they had done it to a family member, Edward took full advantage of his military connections and rooted Marcy out. He wrote back to Williams on September 18, 1866: "I have made inquiries among my acquaintances, in relation to the domicile of the alleged marauder, so far without success. I have no doubt of ultimately succeeding in ferreting him out & in compelling him to make an admission or denial of the charge."[201]

With nothing forthcoming from Marcy for over a year, Edward gave up, leaving Williams fed up. Finally able to contact Marcy directly, Williams fired off a series of letters to him beginning in October 1867, taking the man to task as a plunderer and further demanding that he admit as much. Marcy eventually responded to Williams shortly thereafter, brazenly denying any wrongdoing. "I have been informed that your collection of paintings was destroyed…Middleton Place was burned by detachments of troops belonging to a brigade of which I was Medical Director and it was reported that the destruction was complete including the library and outbuildings." Of course, this was only a half-truth, and both Williams and Marcy knew it. Pressed further in subsequent letters and accusations, Marcy finally relented, conceding that he did have two paintings from Middleton Place but stating the he had only been doing Williams a favor. "I obtained them with no feeling that I was robbing the owner," he wrote, "but that I was trying to save the property from destruction."[202]

Now, whether Marcy actually believed his own absurd statement is irrelevant, and Williams was not listening anyway. Angrily rebutting Marcy's ridiculous excuse, Williams quickly pointed out that if, in fact, Marcy was not a common thief but instead a savior of Middleton Place art, why did he still have it hanging in his house two years later?[203]

Even though Dr. Henry Marcy went to his grave never having admitted "stealing" anything from Middleton Place, he was decent enough to eventually send three of Williams's paintings back by way of a tertiary agent. As for the innumerable publications gathered from the grounds and nearby woods, however, most still sit somewhere in the Harvard University library system—gifts from Marcy to Harvard and still listed in the accession reports there. The "Gentlemen of the Committee for the Examination of the Library" received Marcy's so-called donation on July 13, 1865, and went on to openly record that "Henry Orlando Marcy, M.D. of Cambridgeport has presented several important works which he procured in the rebel states," the "several" being four hundred bound volumes and 2,226 pamphlets and periodicals, all once part of Williams Middleton's library.[204]

Five years after the war, the *Charleston Daily News* editorialized:

> *Though we are five times poorer than before the war, though we have been…plundered and oppressed to a degree which, if continued, will, in a few years more, reduce us to the extreme of poverty, if we do our duty; if we work with willing hearts and hands…I sincerely believe that the hours of every thief and robber in the State will be numbered and that the autumn sun will shine upon a free people.*[205]

Of all the valuables that vanished from Charleston, it is a safe bet that sizeable portions of them no longer remain, at least not in their original form. For sure, plenty of gold and sterling was melted down for cash, while furniture, porcelains and paintings were dashed to pieces. However, for that which was not destroyed for monetary gain or otherwise—that is, what was kept as keepsakes or gifts—it is not as if those items just vanished into thin air.

While what ultimately became of Eliza Wilkinson's shoe buckles, the Trapiers' wedding rings or Charles Manigault's elephant coin remains a mystery, it is still within the realm of possibility that each are still out there…somewhere. All too often, of course, there are the garage sales, flea markets, thrift stores, dumpsters and smelting pots that, if not obliterating an object, do wonders in severing crucial provenances needed for apposite re-identification. Just as quickly as things vanish, though, so too can they reappear, and it is with this hope that many Charlestonians maintain their vigils for these long-lost artifacts, hoping one day to restore them to their proper standing in local history. Indeed, some will be found. Some will not. Others, well, their absence is certainly excusable.

Bay of Naples, attributed to Claude Lorain circa 1641, was one of three paintings eventually returned to Williams Middleton. *Courtesy of Middleton Place Foundation.*

Partial accession record from the Harvard University Library listing Dr. Marcy's gift of books and journals taken from Middleton Place in 1865. *Courtesy of Middleton Place Foundation.*

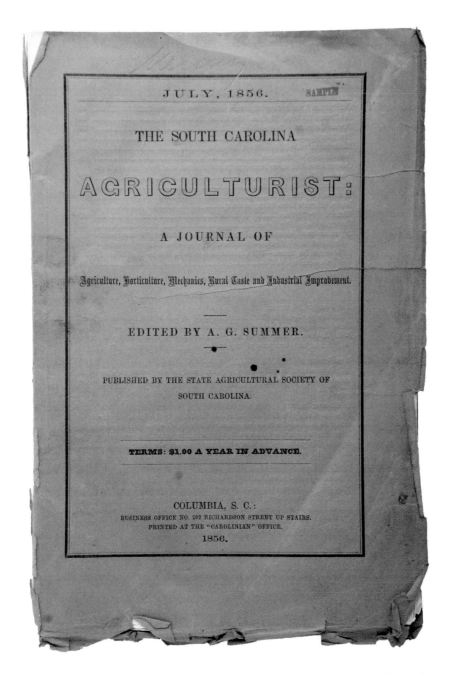

Issue of the July 1856 *South Carolina Agriculturist*, one of several thousand printed items taken from Middleton Place in 1865 and acquisitioned by the Harvard Library. This particular journal was eventually returned to Middleton Place Foundation in 2003. *Courtesy of Middleton Place Foundation.*

When his service to the Confederacy was over—a stint that nearly killed him—William Godber Hinson returned home to James Island and was eventually able to find and excavate his father's 1835 bottle of Madeira, which the old man had buried in the ground and therefore saved from the Yankees. Hinson kept the heirloom wine until 1895, when, on the thirtieth anniversary of the war's end, he drank it.[206]

NOTES

I

1. Though synonymous with "pitcher" or "carafe," the term "flagon" mostly describes a church dispensing vessel.
2. Bonnie Culver McArty, letter to Reverend Edmund G. Coe, December 19, 1944, Church of the Good Shepherd.
3. Burton, *Silversmiths*, xiv.
4. *Random House Dictionary of Americas Popular Proverbs and Sayings*, "To the victor go the spoils."
5. Abbott, *Ghenghis Khan*, 200.
6. Peters, *Public Statutes*, 366.
7. Van Wees, *Status Warriors*, 248; Kassin, Fein and Markus, *Social Psychology*, 307; Burton, *Siege of Charleston*, 324; Conyngham, *Sherman's March*, 314.
8. Ramsay, *History of South-Carolina*, 1:204.
9. Scott et al., *War of the Rebellion*, 34; Trapier, "An Account," 10.
10. Burton, *Siege of Charleston*, 323.
11. Benjamin Huger, letter to Thomas Wells, September 17, 1865, South Caroliniana Library.
12. Sherman, *Memoirs*, 2:368.
13. Whilden, *Recollections*, 4.
14. Ibid.
15. Ada D. Markell, undated letter, MacMeekin family papers, private collection.

16. Schneck, *Burning of Chambersburg*, 26, 58; Bok, *Americanization*, 209.
17. Winthrop, *Military Law*, 2:1,480.
18. Atwood, *Hessians*, 60; Ewald, *Diary*, 202; Borick, *Gallant Defense*, 60–61.
19. Susan H.P. Burn, Papers, Charleston Museum accession file 1946.11.
20. Burton, *Silversmiths*, xiv; Wallace, *History of South Carolina*, 2:201; Ravenel, *Charleston*, 336.

II

21. Modern data suggests that 46 percent of colonial America's wealth was in the South by 1774, with the Chesapeake and New England regions holding only 29 percent and 25 percent, respectively. By the early nineteenth century, most southern capital was tied up in either land (45.9 percent) or black slaves (33.6 percent). Livestock and individual goods were less than 10 percent each. Coclanis, *Shadow*, 125; Warner, *Slavers*, 523; Perkins, *Economy of Colonial America*, 218–21; McCusker and Menard, *Economy of British America*, 60–61.
22. McCusker and Menard, *Economy of British America*, 169; Spriggs et al., *Let It Shine*, 46.
23. Moultrie, *Memoirs*, 354–56.
24. Downs's regrettable faux pas convinced Williamsburg officials to focus the next year's forum exclusively on southern furniture. Niven, "Frank L. Horton," 59; Greenfield, *Out of the Attic*, 50; Rauschenberg and Bivens, *Furniture*, 1:xxvi.
25. McInnis et al., *Refinement*, 1; Reps, *Making of Urban America*, 175.
26. "Official Report" in Snowden and Cutler, *History of South Carolina*, 133–35.
27. Forty shillings in 1761 had about the same purchasing power as $312.05 today; three pounds, ten shillings in 1770, about $492.01 today. Carroll, *Historical Collections*, 343, 511; Rosen, *Short History*, 24.
28. Milligen, "A Short Description" in Edgar, *South Carolina*, 63.
29. With slaves included in his real estate holdings, Heyward's worth adjusts to roughly $54,869,800 today. Phillips, "Slave Labor," 436; Scarborough, *Masters*, 13; Nathaniel Heyward, Papers, South Carolina Historical Society; Arthur Middleton, letter to James Hume, September 19, 1783, Middleton Place Foundation.

30. Borick, *Gallant Defense*, 100–01; Kornblith, *Slavery*, 23.

31. Carroll, *Historical Collections*, 507–08; Eliza Lucas, letter from to Mrs. Boddicott, 1740, in McInnis et al., *Refinement*, 55.

32. *News and Courier*, April 8, 1935.

33. Ravenel, *Charleston*, 91.

34. Hough, *Siege of Charleston*, 57–58.

35. Spruill et al., *South Carolina Women*, 114; Schlesinger, *Colonial Merchants*, 604; Poston, *Buildings of Charleston*, 228–29; Burton, *Siege of Charleston*, 322; Scott et al., *War of the Rebellion*, 2:491; United Daughters of the Confederacy, *Women of the Confederacy*, 166.

36. Twain, *Jumping Frog*, 106.

37. Asbury and Tipple, *Asbury's Journal*, 375.

38. Both the *Columbia Phoenix* and the *Charleston Daily News* attest that the original letter is in the offices of the *Sun and Times* newspaper in Columbus, Georgia, and that "the original is still preserved, and can be shown and substantiated." Yet it appears that no Columbus-based newspaper was *ever* named the *Sun and Times*. This could be a misprint, since there was an Augusta paper known as the *Sun*. Nevertheless, the Myers letter never appeared in it.

39. Of note was a private Thomas Myer (no "s") from Massachusetts in the U.S. Colored Infantry, but he was not listed as anywhere near Camden in February 1865.

40. Hill et al., *Story of One Regiment*, 109; Bostick, *Charleston Under Siege*, 118; Shakespeare, *Henry VI*, act IV, scene 1.

III

41. Wilkinson, *Letters of Eliza Wilkinson*, 9–11.

42. Ibid., 28–30.

43. Richard Lorentz, letter to British Headquarters, March 4, 1780, Charleston Museum Archives, 1991.28.

44. Commager and Morris, *Spirit of Seventy-Six*, 1,068; Weintraub, *Iron Tears*, 62.

45. Weintraub, *Iron Tears*, 221.

46. Ramsay, *History of South-Carolina*, 1:204.

47. Davis, *U.S. Army and Irregular Warfare*, 68; Gordon, *Rise, Progress*, 456–57; Kiel, "War Crimes," 42.

48. Petigru and Carson, *Letters*, 3.

49. *South Carolina Weekly Gazette*, May 31, 1783

50. Not to be confused with Paul Hamilton (1762–1816) of St. Paul's Parish, who fought under Francis Marion and later became secretary of the navy; Cooper and McCord, *Statutes at Large*, 517; Edgar, Bailey and Moore, *Biographical Directory*, 302–03.

51. Ibid.

52. Pulis, *Moving On*, 22.

53. Cooper and McCord, *Statutes at Large*, 517, 519.

54. Edgar, Bailey and Moore, *Biographical Directory*, 303; Memorial of Paul Hamilton.

55. Starke, *Poor Soldier*, 5.

56. *Charleston Mercury Extra*, Charleston Museum Archives, 1941.124.

57. Carey and McDuffie, *"Look Before You Leap,"* 16.

58. Thomas Lynch, letter to Patrick Lynch, July 23, 1863, Charleston Diocesan Archives, item 14W2; Whilden, *Recollections*, 5–6.

59. John Lynch, letter to Louisa Blaine (?), Charleston Diocesan Archives, item 14A10.

60. Lewis, *Camp Life*, 58.

61. Bostick, *Siege of Charleston*, 71; Scott et al., *War of the Rebellion*, 27:11.

62. Robert Gourdin, letter to Andrew Calhoun in Racine, *Gentlemen Merchants*, 580.

63. Ibid.; Johnson, *No Holier Spot*, 28.

64. Simms, *A City Laid Waste*, 9; Charles Holst, letter to friend, March 29, 1864, Charleston Museum Archives.

65. Scott et al., *War of the Rebellion*, 2:797.

66. Pierre Beauregard, letter to Gillmore, August 22, 1863, in Tenney, *Military and Naval History*, 478; Porter, *Led On*, 152; *Charleston Mercury*, February 4, 1865.

67. Simms, *A City Laid Waste*, 8.

68. *Columbia Phoenix*, May 10, 1865.

69. Simms, *A City Laid Waste*, 8.

70. Grant, *Personal Memoirs*, 588.

71. Nichols, *Story of the Great March*, 152–53.

IV

72. Sherman, *Memoirs*, 2:254.

73. Bostick, *Sunken Plantations*, 83.

74. Charleston Museum accession file 1982.150; Henrietta Macbeth, letter to family member, Charleston Museum accession file 2008.33.

75. Ibid.

76. "Fort Sumter Copy Book," Charleston Museum Archives, 1989.14.

77. Charleston Museum accession file 2004.60.

78. Moore, *Diary of the Revolution*, 800; Chestnut and Williams, *Diary from Dixie*, 380.

79. Borick, *Gallant Defense*, 152; Papers of Henry Laurens, 15:287.

80. "Draught of Part of the Province of South Carolina Showing the March & Encampments of the British Troops…1779," William L. Clements Library, University of Michigan; Borick, *Gallant Defense*, 61–63; Preservations Consultants Inc., "Survey Report," 18.

81. Charleston Museum accession file 1972.33; Dill, "Dills Family," 31–32; Anthony, "Dill Sanctuary."

82. Wallace, *History of South Carolina*, 1:38; Coffin, *Freedom Triumphant*, 4:308; Whilden, *Recollections*, 11.

83. Sass and Ball, "Comingtee Treasure," 28.

84. Will of Lila K.T. Johnson, November 6, 1974, Charleston Museum accession file 1985.32.

85. Troops plundered nearly everything the Trapiers did *not* bury, including "the gold seal of Reverend Trapier's grandfather and a brooch containing the hair of Mrs. Trapier's late father." Trapier, "An Account," 8; Stokes, *Civilians*, 74–75.

86. Emerson, *Sons of Privilege*, 58; Stokes, *Civilians*, 78–79.

87. Manigault's family exhumed Alfred's body (again) the following year and reinterred it at St. Philip's churchyard in Charleston. Manigault, Family Papers; Stokes, *Civilians*, 78–79.

88. Parole pass of Gabriel Manigault, June 21, 1780; Manigault, War Journal.

89. Manigault, Family Papers; Batson and Sawyer, *Louis Manigault*, 3, 43–44.

90. Manigault, Family Papers; Manigault, War Journal; Batson and Sawyer, *Louis Manigault*, 85; J.W. Bandy, letter to Louis Manigault, May 1, 1865; Manigault, Plantation Journal, 59.

91. J.W. Bandy, letter to Louis Manigault, May 1, 1865; Manigault, Plantation Journal, 55–71.

92. Manigault, Family Papers.

93. Manigault, War Journal.

94. Franklin and Mikula, *South Carolina Plantations*, 91; Mazyck, *Charleston Museum*, 20; Ravenel, "Report, August 27, 1866."

95. Gilt meaning a far less valuable false-gold plating, comparable to brass. Chestnut and Williams, *Diary from Dixie*, 389.

96. Sarah Lowndes did mention that she had served the soldiers "plenty of drink," which likely helped dissuade their initial intentions of looting the house. Sarah Lowndes, letter to Rawlins Lowndes, May 17, 1780, in Clinton papers.

97. Johnson, *Traditions and Reminiscences*, 381–82.

V

98. Sherman, *Memoirs*, 2:175.

99. Scott et al., *War of the Rebellion*, 28:12.

100. Barton, *Red Cross*, 13.

101. Winthrop, *Military Law and Precedents*, 2:1, 412; Moultrie, *Memoirs*, 2:251–52.

102. Tokar, "Logistics," 42.

103. Lee, *Memoirs of the War*, 145.

104. Taylor, *Supply for Tomorrow*, 119; Coggins, *Arms and Equipment*, 121; Finseth, *American Civil War*, 171; Burrows, "'Left to Our Fate,'" 74.

105. Finseth, *American Civil War*, 171; Coggins, *Arms and Equipment*, 170.

106. Wilkinson, *Letters*, 88; Chesney, "Journal," 22–25; Arthur Middleton, Papers, 1742–1787, Middleton Place Foundation.

107. Williams Middleton, letter to Eliza, July 8, 1854, Middleton Place Foundation.

108. Ibid., letter to W.D. Clancy, November, 29, 1870, Middleton Place Foundation.

109. Ibid., letter to Jane Pringle, September 27, 1870, Middleton Place Foundation.

110. Ibid., letter to W.D. Clancy, November, 29, 1870, Middleton Place Foundation.

111. Kerr, *Civil War Surgeon*, 206; Zierden, Smith and Anthony, "Our Duty."

112. Ibid.

113. Ibid.

114. Ibid.; Doyle, *New Men*, 227–28.

115. Flexner, *Traitor and the Spy*, 264; Faust and Delaney, *Historical Times*, 95; Thomas Ferguson, letter to John P. Hatch, June 26, 1865, College of Charleston Special Collections Library.

116. Wallace, *History of South Carolina*, 3:205; Dwight, "Bummers," 390.

117. Wells, *Charleston Light Dragoons*, 83.

118. Chestnut and Williams, *Diary from Dixie*, 369.

119. Wells, *Charleston Light Dragoons*, 86.

120. Brooks, *Butler and His Cavalry*, 470; Wells, *Charleston Light Dragoons*, 87.

121. Nichols, *Story of the Great March*, 181; William Sherman, letter to Wade Hampton, February 24, 1865, in Moore, *Rebellion Record*, 387.

122. Wade Hampton, letter to William Sherman, February 27, 1865, in Moore, *Rebellion Record*, 387.

123. West Point Rice Mill records, 1860–1925, (1201.00) South Carolina Historical Society; Powers, *Black Charlestonians*, 101.

124. Ramsay, *History of South-Carolina*, 2:179.

VI

125. Dalcho, *Historical Account*, 32; Calhoun, "Scourging Wrath."

126. Hewatt, *Historical Account*, 1:143.

127. Mazyck, *Charleston Museum*, 6.

128. An additional noteworthy fire on April 24, 1838, burned down most of Charleston's merchant corridor, costing thousands in goods. *Charleston Courier*, April 26, 1838; Cardozo, *Reminiscences*, 28–29; Hicks, *City of Ruin*, 87–88; Burton, *Siege of Charleston*, 82; McInnis, *Politics of Taste*, 98.

129. Ramsay, *History of South-Carolina*, 2:100.

130. Fraser, *Hurricanes*, 14–20, 50, 80; *South Carolina Gazette*, September 19, 1752.

131. Fraser, *Hurricanes*, 50; Louis Manigault, Papers.

132. Ramsay, *History of South-Carolina*, 2:305; McKinley, *Earthquake*, 6, 32–33.

133. John 8:7.

134. William Henderson, letter to John Rutledge in Rankin, *Francis Marion*, 233; Johnson, *Life of Greene*, 2:211; Lanning, *African Americans*, 71–72; Lanning, *American Revolution*, 100, 292–93.

135. Ward, *Washington's Enforcers*, 105–06.

136. Borick, *Gallant Defense*, 92–93.

137. Webber, "Order Book"; Moss, *Roster of South Carolina Patriots*, 2:1,010; Lossing, *Pictorial Field-Book*, 687–89; Russell, *American Revolution*, 242.

138. Chestnut and Williams, *Diary from Dixie*, 155; Charleston Museum accession files 1987.60 and 1986.11

139. Wise, *Lifeline of the Confederacy*, 121.

140. The saddle was declared "confiscated goods" and subsequently auctioned off to Lieutenant Colonel Charles M. Wheldon. In 1910, Wheldon's widow presented the saddle to the Ancient and Honorable Artillery Company of Massachusetts, of which her late husband was a member. Ancient and Honorable Artillery Company of Massachusetts accession file.

141. Wise, *Lifeline of the Confederacy*, 124.

142. Charles Holst, letter to friend, Charleston Museum Archives.

143. Burton, *Siege of Charleston*, 317–20; *Charleston Courier*, February 20, 1865.

144. Several sources, including Burton, conclude that the fire spread as a result of several young boys entertaining themselves by throwing handfuls of gunpowder, gathered from the kegs in the adjacent room, into the cotton fires. Burton, *Siege of Charleston*, 320–21.

145. Dufort, "Charleston During the Siege" in *Our Women in the War*, 52; Cramer, Diary, 1865–1868, (34/45) South Carolina Historical Society.

146. Louis Manigault, Papers; Batson and Sawyers, *Louis Manigault*, 113.

147. *Charleston Daily News*, May 23, 1866.

148. Ibid., February 23, 1867; *Daily Phoenix*, February 23, 1867.

149. Williams Middleton, letter to Eliza, September 28, 1870, Middleton Place Foundation.

150. Catalogue of Fifth Avenue Auction Rooms, Lot 176, Charleston Museum Archives.

VII

151. *Journal of the Annual Convention*, 91.

152. Dalcho, *Historical Account*, 263.

153. Nelson, *Beauty of Holiness*, 335.

154. Förster and Nagler, *On the Road*, 165.

155. Vestry minutes St. John's Colleton in Nelson, *Beauty of Holiness*, 333.

156. Gilman et al, *Old and the New*, 11; Cornelian Hancock, letter, Mount Pleasant Presbyterian Church Library.

157. Charleston Museum loan file IL1996.6

158. *Journal of the Annual Convention*, 84–85.

159. Ibid., 85.

160. Cardozo, *Reminiscences*, 40–41.

161. Woodmason, *Carolina Backcountry*, 72; Nelson, *Beauty of Holiness*, 48; Johnson, *Traditions and Reminiscences*, 175–76.

162. Recent evidence suggests that although McPhersonville was again sacked by Union forces in 1865, Sheldon Church was left badly damaged but unburned. Lossing, *Pictorial Field-Book*, 761; Rowland, Moore and Rogers, *History of Beaufort County*, 175.

163. Johnson, *Life and Letters of Benjamin Morgan Palmer*, 25.

164. Johnson, *Traditions and Reminiscences*, 175.

165. Francis Marion, letter, December 23, 1779, private collection; Rowland, Moore and Rogers, *History of Beaufort County*, 208.

166. Ramsay, *History of South-Carolina*, 1:179; *Journal of the Annual Convention*, 84; Williams Middleton, letter to Jane Pringle, September 27, 1870, Middleton Place Foundation.

167. Porter, *Led On*, 153–54.

168. Smith, *Righteous Community*, 23, 166.

169. Smith, "Baronies of South Carolina," 34–35; Hough *Siege of Charleston*, 109; *South Carolina Gazette*, July 12, 1783.

170. *Silver of St. Philip's Church*, 5, 12.

171. Ibid.

172. Clute, *Annals and Parish Register*, 16; Smith, *Righteous Community*, 24–25.

173. *Journal of the Annual Convention*, 84.

174. Nelson, *Beauty of Holiness*, 333.

175. By the turn of the twentieth century, most American Presbyterian clerics considered communion a work of grace and not so much a prize for a

pious performance and let go of the token tradition. Bason, *Communion Tokens*, 64; Tenney, *Communion Tokens*, 101.

176. Two silver and three pewter; Lilly, *Beyond the Burning Bush*, 14–15.

177. Another silver token turned up at public auction in 2004, and the Presbyterian Historical Society in Philadelphia holds both a silver and pewter First (Scots) communion token in its permanent collection. Lilly, *Beyond the Burning* Bush, 14–15.

VIII

178. Charleston Museum accession file 1973.89.

179. Ibid.

180. Edgar, *Encyclopedia of South Carolina*, 81.

181. Wallace, *Henry Laurens*, 426.

182. Ibid., 67–68.

183. Burton, *Silversmiths*, 21–22.

184. Dr. Robert Ball Jr., Jeff Ball interviews with the author.

185. Sass and Ball, "Comingtee Treasure," 142.

186. Ibid.

187. Ibid.

188. Ibid.; Martha Sullivan, interview with Drew Ruddy, April 2, 2013.

189. Ibid.

190. Martha Sullivan, interview with Drew Ruddy, April 2, 2013.

191. Ibid.

192. Charlotte Morris Manigault, letter, private collection.

193. Grimball family papers, 1683–1930, UNC Libraries collection number 00980; Gailor, *Some Memories*, 132; Charlotte Morris Manigault, letter, private collection.

194. Charlotte Morris Manigault, letter, private collection.

195. Ibid.

196. Trimpi, *Crimson Confederates*, 175; *Charleston Daily News*, December 22, 1866.

197. Martha Kirk, letter to Peter C. Gaillard, September 4, 1886, private collection.

198. Henrietta Aiken Rhett, letter to Charles Simonton, September 28, 1866, Rhett family papers, Charleston Museum Archives.

199. Manigault Papers.

200. Despite his claim to taking "small" paintings, each was approximately thirty by forty-two inches. Marcy, *Diary*, South Carolina Historical Society.

201. Williams Middleton, letter to Eliza Middleton Fisher, September 16, 1866, Middleton Place Foundation; Edward Middleton, letter to Williams Middleton, September 18, 1866, Middleton Place Foundation

202. Cheves and Greene, "Robbing the Owner," 100.

203. Williams Middleton, letter to Henry Marcy, October 22, 1867, Middleton Place Foundation.

204. Harvard accession records, 1866; (VAIII 50.5), Middleton Place Foundation; John Sibley, Harvard University Library Reports, 1856–1877, Middleton Place Foundation.

205. *Charleston Daily News*, July 7, 1870.

206. Bonstelle and Buxton, *James Island*, 31.

BIBLIOGRAPHY

Abbott, Jacob. *History of Genghis Khan.* New York: Harper Brothers, 1860.

All, John L. *A Stately Heritage: The Story of Mount Pleasant Presbyterian Church, 1699–1996.* Charleston, SC: R.L. Bryan Company, 2001.

Anthony, Ronald W. "Dill Sanctuary Archaeology: A Descriptive Summary." *Archaeological Contributions* 46 (July 2012).

Asbury, Francis, and Ezra Squier Tipple. *The Heart of Asbury's Journal.* New York: Methodist Book Concern, 1904.

Atwood, Rodney. *The Hessians.* Cambridge, MA: Cambridge University Press, 1980.

Barnett, Bert. "'The Severest and Bloodiest Artillery I Ever Saw:'" Colonel E.P. Alexander and the First Corps Artillery Assail the Peach Orchard July 2, 1863." Gettysburg Seminar, National Park Service E-Library. http://www.nps.gov/history/history/online_books/gett/gettysburg_seminars/7/essay4.pdf (accessed August 23, 2013).

Barton, Clara. *The Red Cross in Peace and War.* N.p.: American Historical Press, 1899.

Bason, Autence A. *Communion Tokens of the United States of America*. Greensboro, NC: A.A. Bason, 1989.

Batson, Annie Jenkins, and Lindell Sawyers. *Louis Manigault: Gentleman from South Carolina*. Roswell, GA: Wolfe, 1995.

Biographical and Genealogical Research on Nathaniel Heyward. Charleston: (30-4 Heyward) South Carolina Historical Society.

Bok, Edward William. *The Americanization of Edward Bok: The Autobiography of a Dutch Boy Fifty Years After*. Auckland, NZ: Floating Press, 1920.

Bonstelle, Carolyn Ackerly, and Geordie Buxton. *James Island*. Charleston, SC: Arcadia, 2008.

Borick, Carl P. *A Gallant Defense: The Siege of Charleston, 1780*. Columbia: University of South Carolina Press, 2003.

Bostick, Douglas W. *Charleston Under Siege: The Impregnable City*. Charleston, SC: The History Press, 2010.

———. *Sunken Plantations: The Santee Cooper Project*. Charleston, SC: The History Press, 2008.

Brooks, U.R. *Butler and His Cavalry in the War of Secession, 1861–1865*. Columbia, SC: State Co., 1909.

Buhk, Tobin T. *True Crime in the Civil War: Cases of Murder, Treason, Counterfeiting, Massacre, Plunder and Abuse*. Mechanicsburg, PA: Stackpole Books, 2012.

Burrows, Sarah E., PhD. "'Left to Our Fate:' South Carolina Women During the Civil War and Reconstruction." PhD thesis, University of South Carolina, 2008.

Burton, E. Milby. *The Siege of Charleston, 1861–1865*. Columbia: University of South Carolina Press, 1970.

———. *South Carolina Silversmiths, 1690–1860*. Rutland, VT: C. Tuttle Co., 1968.

Calhoun, Jeanne A. "The Scourging Wrath of God:" Early Hurricanes in Charleston, 1700–1804. *Charleston Museum Leaflet* 29. Charleston, SC: Charleston Museum, 1983.

Cardozo, Jacob N. *Reminiscences of Charleston.* Charleston, SC: J. Walker, 1866.

Carey, Mathew, and George McDuffie. *"Look Before You Leap": Addresses to the Citizens of the Southern States.* Philadelphia: Haswell & Barrington, 1835.

Carroll, B.R. *Historical Collections of South Carolina.* New York: Harper & Bros., 1836.

Chesney, Alexander, and Wilbur H. Siebert. "The Journal of Alexander Chesney, a South Carolina Loyalist in the Revolution and After." *The Ohio State University Bulletin* 26, no. 4 (1921): 1–56.

Chesnut, Mary Boykin Miller, and Ben Ames Williams. *A Diary from Dixie.* New York: D. Appleton & Co., 1905.

Clinton, Sir Henry. Papers. William L. Clements Library, University of Michigan, Ann Arbor.

Clute, Robert F. *The Annals and Parish Register of St. Thomas and St. Denis Parish, in South Carolina, from 1680 to 1884.* Charleston, SC: Walker, Evans & Cogswell, 1884.

Coclanis, Peter A. *The Shadow of a Dream: Economic Life and Death in the South Carolina Low Country, 1670–1920.* New York: Oxford University Press, 1989.

Coffin, Charles Carleton. *Freedom Triumphant: The Fourth Period of the War of the Rebellion from September 1864 to Its Close.* New York: Harper & Bros., 1891.

Coggins, Jack. *Arms and Equipment of the Civil War.* Garden City, NY: Doubleday, 1962.

Collections of the Ancient and Honorable Artillery Company of Massachusetts, Boston. (Contain documentation concerning General P.G.T. Beauregard's saddle.)

Collections of the Charleston Museum, Charleston, SC. (Contain a number of documents and related material discussing looted objects and family provenances.)

Collections of the Diocesan Archives, the Catholic Diocese of Charleston, Charleston, SC. (Containing documents relating to the Lynch family's experiences during the Civil War.)

Collections of Middleton Place Foundation, Charleston, SC. (Containing documents relating to the Middleton family's experiences during the American Revolution and the Civil War.)

Commager, Henry Steele, and Richard B. Morris, eds. *The Spirit of Seventy-Six*. New York: Harper & Row, 1967.

Conyngham, David Power. *Sherman's March through the South with Sketches and Incidents of the Campaign*. New York: Sheldon and Co., 1865.

Cooper, Thomas, and David James McCord. *The Statutes at Large of South Carolina*. Columbia, SC: A.S. Johnston, 1836.

Cramer, Adolph. "Adolph F.C. Cramer Diary 1865–1868." Charleston: (34/45) South Carolina Historical Society.

Dalcho, Frederick. *An Historical Account of the Protestant Episcopal Church in South-Carolina*. Charleston, SC: E. Miller, 1820.

Davis, Richard G. *The U.S. Army and Irregular Warfare, 1775–2007*. Washington, D.C.: Center of Military History/United States Army, 2008.

Doyle, Don Harrison. *New Men, New Cities, New South: Atlanta, Nashville, Charleston, Mobile, 1860–1910*. Chapel Hill: University of North Carolina Press, 1990.

"Draught of Part of the Province of South Carolina Showing the March & Encampments of the British Troops: 1779." William L. Clements Library, University of Michigan.

Dufort, Pauline. "Charleston During the Siege." In *Our Women in the War*. Charleston, SC: News and Courier Book Presses, 1885.

Dwight, Henry O. "Bummers in Sherman's Army." *Beadles Magazine* 1, no. 25 (1866): 389–98.

Edgar, Walter B. *South Carolina: A History*. Columbia: University of South Carolina Press, 1998.

Edgar, Walter B., ed. *The South Carolina Encyclopedia*. 2nd ed. Columbia: University of South Carolina Press, 2006.

Edgar, Walter B., N. Louise Bailey and Alexander Moore. *Biographical Directory of the South Carolina House of Representatives*. Columbia: University of South Carolina Press, 1974.

Emerson, W. Eric. *Sons of Privilege: The Charleston Light Dragoons in the Civil War*. Columbia: University of South Carolina Press, 2005.

Ewald, Johann von, and Joseph P. Tustin. *Diary of the American War: A Hessian Journal*. New Haven, CT: Yale University Press, 1979.

Faust, Patricia L., and Norman C. Delaney. *Historical Times Illustrated Encyclopedia of the Civil War*. New York: Harper & Row, 1986.

Finseth, Ian Frederick. *The American Civil War: An Anthology of Essential Writings*. New York: Routledge, 2006.

Flexner, James T. *The Traitor and the Spy: Benedict Arnold and John André*. New York: Harcourt, Brace & World, 1953.

Förster, Stig, and Jorg Nagler. *On the Road to Total War: The American Civil War and the German Wars of Unification, 1861–1871*. Washington, D.C.: German Historical Institute, 1997.

Franklin, Paul, and Nancy Mikula. *South Carolina's Plantations & Historic Homes*. Minneapolis, MN: Voyageur Press, 2006.

Fraser, Walter J. *Lowcountry Hurricanes: Three Centuries of Storms at Sea and Ashore*. Athens: University of Georgia Press, 2006.

Gailor, Thomas Frank. *Some Memories*. Kingsport, TN: Southern Publishers, 1937.

Gilman, Samuel, et al. *The Old and the New; or, Discourses and Proceedings at the Dedication of the Re-modelled Unitarian Church in Charleston*. Charleston, SC: Samuel G. Courtenay, 1854.

Gordon, William. *The History of the Rise, Progress, and Establishment of the Independence of the United States of America*. 2nd ed. New York: Samuel Campbell, 1794.

Grant, Ulysses S. *Personal Memoirs of U.S. Grant*. 2 vols. New York: Charles L. Webster & Co., 1894.

Greenberg, Kenneth S. *The Second American Revolution: South Carolina Politics, Society, and Secession, 1776–1860*. Madison: University of Wisconsin Press, 1976.

Greenfield, Briann G. *Out of the Attic: Inventing Antiques in Twentieth-Century New England*. Amherst: University of Massachusetts Press, 2009.

Hancock, Cornelia. Papers. Mount Pleasant Presbyterian Church Library, Mount Pleasant, SC.

Heidler, David Stephen, and Jeanne T. Heidler, eds. *Encyclopedia of the American Civil War: A Political, Social, and Military History*. New York: W.W. Norton & Company Inc., 2000.

Hewatt, Alexander. *An Historical Account of the Rise and Progress of the Colonies of South Carolina and Georgia*. 2 vols. London: 1779.

Heyward, Nathaniel, and Thomas B. Ferguson. Family Papers. College of Charleston Special Collections Library, Charleston, SC.

Hicks, Brian. *City of Ruin: Charleston at War 1860–1865*. Charleston, SC: Evening Post Books, 2012.

Hill, J.A., et al. *The Story of One Regiment: The Eleventh Maine Infantry Volunteers in the War of the Rebellion*. New York: J.J. Little & Co., 1896.

Hough, Franklin Benjamin. *The Siege of Charleston...Including Biographical Sketches, Incidents, and Anecdotes...Particularly of Residents in the Upper Country.* Charleston, SC: Walker & James, 1851.

Johnson, Joseph. *Traditions and Reminiscences, Chiefly of the American Revolution in the South.* Charleston, SC: Walker & James, 1851.

Johnson, Kristina Dunn. *No Holier Spot of Ground: Confederate Monuments and Cemeteries of South Carolina.* Charleston, SC: The History Press, 2009.

Johnson, Thomas C. *The Life and Letters of Benjamin Morgan Palmer.* Richmond, VA: Presbyterian Committee of Publication, 1906.

Johnson, William. *Sketches of the Life and Correspondence of Nathanael Greene.* Charleston, SC: A.E. Miller, 1822.

Johnston, George Milligen. *A Short Description of the Province of South-Carolina, with an Account of the Air, Weather, and Diseases, at Charles-Town.* London: John Hinton, 1770.

Journal of the Proceedings of the Seventy-Eighth Annual Convention of the Protestant Episcopal Church in South Carolina. Charleston, SC: Joseph Walker, 1868.

Kassin, Saul, Steven Fein and Hazel Rose Markus. *Social Psychology.* Stamford, CT: Cengage Learning, 2013.

Kerr, Paul B. *Civil War Surgeon: A Biography of James Langstaff Dunn, MD.* Bloomington, IN: AuthorHouse, 2005.

Kiel, John L., Jr. "War Crimes in the American Revolution: Examining the Conduct of Lt. Col. Banastre Tarleton and the British Legion during the Southern Campaigns of 1780–1781." *Military Law Review* 213 (2012): 29–64.

Kirk, Martha. Papers. Private collection.

Kirkland, Randolph W. *Dark Hours: South Carolina Soldiers, Sailors and Citizens Held in Federal Prisons, 1860–1865.* Columbia: University of South Carolina Press, 2002.

Kornblith, Gary John. *Slavery and Sectional Strife in the Early American Republic, 1776–1821*. Lanham, MD: Rowman & Littlefield, 2010.

Lanning, Michael Lee. *African Americans in the Revolutionary War*. New York: Citadel Press, 2005.

———. *The American Revolution 100: The People, Battles, and Events of the American War for Independence, Ranked by Their Significance*. Naperville, IL: Sourcebooks, 2008.

Laurens, Henry. Papers. Henry W. Kendall Collection. South Caroliniana Library, University of South Carolina, Columbia.

Lee, Henry. *Memoirs of the War in the Southern Department*. 2 vols. Philadelphia: Bradsford and Inskeep, 1812.

Leleand, Harriott C., and Harlan Greene. "Robbing the Owner or Saving the Property from Destruction?" *South Carolina Historical and Genealogical Magazine* 78, no. 2 (1977): 92–103.

Lewis, Richard. *Camp Life of a Confederate Boy, of Bratton's Brigade, Longstreet's Corps, C.S.A.* Charleston, SC: News and Courier Book Presses, 1888.

Lilly, Edward G. *Beyond the Burning Bush: First (Scots) Presbyterian Church, Charleston, S.C.* Charleston, SC: Garnier, 1971.

Lincoln, Benjamin. *Original Papers Relating to the Siege of Charleston, 1780*. Charleston, SC: Walker, Evans & Cogswell, 1898.

Lossing, Benson John. *The Pictorial Field-Book of the Revolution; or, Illustrations, by Pen and Pencil, of the History, Biography, Scenery, Relics, and Traditions of the War for Independence*. New York: Harper & Bros., 1851.

Lowndes, Rawlins. Papers. William L. Clements Library, University of Michigan, Ann Arbor.

Manigault, Gabriel. Plantation Journal. Manigault Family Papers #484, Southern Historical Collection, Wilson Library, University of North Carolina at Chapel Hill.

Manigault, Louis. War Journal. Private collection.

———. Papers. Private collection.

Marcy, Henry O. *Diary of a Surgeon, 1864–1899*. (34/496) South Carolina Historical Society.

Mazyck, William Gaillard. *The Charleston Museum, Its Genesis and Development*. Charleston, SC: Walker, Evans & Cogswell, 1908.

McCusker, John J., and Russell R. Menard. *The Economy of British America, 1607–1789*. Chapel Hill: University of North Carolina Press, 1985.

McInnis, Maurie D., et al. *In Pursuit of Refinement: Charlestonians Abroad, 1740–1860*. Columbia: University of South Carolina Press, 1999.

McInnis, Maurie D. *The Politics of Taste in Antebellum Charleston*. Chapel Hill: University of North Carolina Press, 2005.

McKinley, Carlyle. *A Descriptive Narrative of the Earthquake of August 31, 1886: Prepared Expressly for the City Year Book, 1886*. Charleston, SC: Walker, Evans & Cogswell, 1887.

Memorial of Paul Hamilton in "Commission of Enquiry into the Losses and Services of American Loyalists, Transcripts, American Loyalists Collection, 1777–1790." 74 vols. Manuscripts and Archives Division, New York Public Library.

Montgomery, Louisa, and Charlotte Morris Manigault. Papers. Private collection.

Moore, Frank. *Diary of the American Revolution from Newspapers and Original Documents*. New York: C.T. Evans, 1863.

———. *The Rebellion Record; a Diary of American Events…Incidents, Poetry, Etc.* New York: D. Van Nostrand, 1868.

Moss, Bobby. *Roster of South Carolina Patriots in the American Revolution*. Vol. 2. Baltimore, MD: Genealogical Publishing Company, 1983.

Moultrie, William. *Memoirs of the American Revolution So Far as It Related to the States of North and South Carolina, and Georgia*. Vol. 2. New York: D. Longworth, 1802.

Nelson, Louis P. *The Beauty of Holiness: Anglicanism & Architecture in Colonial South Carolina*. Chapel Hill: University of North Carolina Press, 2008.

Nichols, George Ward. *The Story of the Great March*. New York: Harper & Bros., 1865.

Niven, Penelope. "Frank L. Horton and the Roads to MESDA." *Journal of Early Southern Decorative Arts* 27 (2001): 1–136.

Perkins, Edwin J. *The Economy of Colonial America*. 2nd ed. New York: Columbia University Press, 1980.

Peters, Richard. *The Public Statutes at Large of the United States of America, from the Organization of the Government in 1789, to March 3, 1845*. Boston: C.C. Little and J. Brown, 1845.

Petigru, James L., and James Carson. *Life, Letters and Speeches of James Louis Petigru: The Union Man of the South*. Washington, D.C.: W.H. Lowdermilk & Co., 1920.

Phillips, Ulrich B. "The Slave Labor Problem in the Charleston District." *Political Science Quarterly* 22, no. 3 (1907): 416–39.

Porter, Anthony T. *Led On! Step by Step: Scenes from Clerical, Military, Educational, and Plantation Life in the South, 1828–1898. An Autobiography*. New York: G.P. Putnam's Sons, 1898.

Poston, Jonathan H. *The Buildings of Charleston: A Guide to the City's Architecture*. Columbia: University of South Carolina Press, 1997.

Powers, Bernard Edward. *Black Charlestonians: A Social History, 1822–1885*. Fayetteville: University of Arkansas Press, 1994.

Preservation Consultants Inc. "Survey Report: James Island and Johns Island Historical and Architectural Inventory." Project carried out for South

Carolina Department of Archives and History, the City of Charleston and Charleston County. http://nationalregister.sc.gov/SurveyReports/HC10002.pdf.

Pulis, John W. *Moving On: Black Loyalists in the Afro-Atlantic World*. New York: Garland, 1999.

Racine, Philip. *Gentlemen Merchants: A Charleston Family's Odyssey, 1828–1870*. Knoxville: University of Tennessee Press, 2008.

Ramsay, David. *History of South-Carolina, from Its First Settlement in 1670 to the Year 1808*. 2 vols. Charleston: David Longworth, 1809.

Rankin, Hugh F. *Francis Marion: The Swamp Fox*. N.p.: Crowell, 1973.

Rauschenberg, Bradford L., and John Bivins. *The Furniture of Charleston, 1680–1820*. 3 vols. Winston-Salem, NC: Old Salem Inc., 2003.

Ravenel, Daniel. "Report by Mr. Daniel Ravenel, President of the Board of Trustees of the College, August, 27, 1866." Charleston Museum Archives.

Ravenel, Harriott Horry. *Charleston: The Place and the People*. New York: Macmillan Co., 1906.

Reps, John William. *The Making of Urban America: A History of City Planning in the United States*. Princeton, NJ: Princeton University Press, 1965.

Rosen, Robert N. *Confederate Charleston: An Illustrated History of the City and the People During the Civil War*. Columbia: University of South Carolina Press, 1994.

———. *A Short History of Charleston*. San Francisco: Lexikos, 1982.

Rowland, Lawrence Sanders, Alexander Moore and George C. Rogers. *The History of Beaufort County, South Carolina*. Columbia: University of South Carolina Press, 1996.

Russell, David Lee. *The American Revolution in the Southern Colonies*. Jefferson, NC: McFarland & Co., 2000.

Sass, Herbert R., and Charlotte Ball. "How the Comingtee Treasure Was Found." *Saturday Evening Post* 219, no. 51 (1947): 28–29, 140–44.

Scarborough, William K. *Masters of the Big House: Elite Slaveholders of the Mid-Nineteenth-Century South.* Baton Rouge: Louisiana State University Press, 2006.

Schlesinger, Arthur M. *The Colonial Merchants and the American Revolution, 1763–1776.* New York: F. Ungar Pub. Co., 1957.

Schneck, B.S. *The Burning of Chambersburg, Pennsylvania.* Philadelphia: Lindsay & Blakiston, 1865.

Scott, Robert N. et al., eds. *The War of the Rebellion: A Compilation of the Official Records of the Union and Confederate Armies.* Washington, D.C.: Government Printing Office, 1880.

Shakespeare, William. *The Works of Shakespeare in Seven Volumes.* Edited by Lewis Theobald. London: Bettesworth and Hitch, 1733.

Sherman, William Tecumseh. *Memoirs of General William T. Sherman.* 2 vols. New York: D. Appleton & Co., 1875.

The Silver of St. Philip's Church, Charles Town, Charleston: 1670–1970. Charleston, SC: St. Philip's Church, 1970.

Simms, William Gilmore. *A City Laid Waste: The Sack and Destruction of the City of Columbia, S.C.* Columbia, SC: Power Press of Daily Phoenix, 1865.

———. *South-Carolina in the Revolutionary War.* Charleston, SC: Walker and James, 1853.

Smith, Bruce. "Water Buffalo Come Home to S.C.'s Middleton Place." *USA Today*, October 4, 2007.

Smith, Henry A.M., "The Baronies of South Carolina." *South Carolina Historical and Genealogical Magazine* 18, no.1 (1917): 13–36.

Smith, Robert. *The American Revolution and Righteous Community: Selected Sermons of Bishop Robert Smith.* Edited by Charles Wilbanks. Columbia: University of South Carolina Press, 2007.

Smith, Thomas. Papers, 1856–1907. (SCU.SCL.M.0006) South Caroliniana Library, University of South Carolina.

Smythe, Louisa McCord. *Recollections of Louisa Rebecca Hayne McCord.* Charleston Museum Archives.

Snowden, Yates, and H.G. Cutler. *History of South Carolina.* 5 vols. New York: Lewis Publishing Co., 1920.

Spriggs, Lynne E. et al. *Let It Shine: Self-Taught Art from the T. Marshall Hahn Collection.* Atlanta, GA: High Museum of Art, 2001.

Spruill, Marjorie J., Valinda Littlefield and Joan Johnson. *South Carolina Women: Their Lives and Times.* Vol. 1. Athens: University of Georgia Press, 2009.

Starke, Mariana. *The Poor Soldier: An American Tale Founded on a Recent Fact.* 2nd ed. London: J. Walter, 1789.

Stokes, Karen. *South Carolina Civilians in Sherman's Path: Stories of Courage amid Civil War Destruction.* Charleston, SC: The History Press, 2012.

Stowell, Ellery C., and Henry F. Munro. *International Cases, Arbitrations and Incidents Illustrative of International Law as Practiced by Independent States.* Boston: Houghton Mifflin Company, 1916.

Sullivan, Martha. Interview by Drew Ruddy, April 2, 2013. The South Caroliniana Library and the South Carolina Artifact and Documentation Project, Columbia.

Tarleton, Banastre. *A History of the Campaigns of 1780 and 1781: In the Southern Provinces of North America.* Dublin, IR: Colles, 1787.

Taylor, Lenette S. *"The Supply for Tomorrow Must Not Fail:" The Civil War Captain Simon Perkins, Jr., a Union Quartermaster.* Kent, OH: Kent State University Press, 2004.

Taylor, Thomas, and Sallie Enders Conner. *South Carolina Women in the Confederacy*. Columbia, SC: State Co., 1903.

Tenney, Samuel Mills. *Communion Tokens: Their Origin, History, and Use, with a Treatise on the Relation of the Sacrament to the Vitality and Revivals of the Church*. Grand Rapids, MI: Zondervan Publishing House, 1936.

Tenney, William Jewett. *The Military and Naval History of the Rebellion in the United States, with Biographical Sketches of Deceased Officers*. New York: D. Appleton & Company, 1865.

Titelman, Gregory. *Random House Dictionary of America's Popular Proverbs and Sayings*. 2nd ed. New York: Random House, 2000.

Tokar, John A. "Logistics and the British Defeat in the Revolutionary War." *Army Logistician* 31, no. 5 (1999): 42.

Trapier, Sarah Dehon. "Gadsden Allied Family Papers, 1703–1939." Charleston: (1032.03) South Carolina Historical Society.

Trimpi, Helen P. *Crimson Confederates: Harvard Men Who Fought for the South*. Knoxville: University of Tennessee Press, 2010.

Twain, Mark. *The Jumping Frog and 18 Other Stories*. Reprint. Escondido, CA: Book Tree, 2000.

Tyler, Mason Whiting, and William Seymour Tyler. *Recollections of the Civil War; with Many Original Diary Entries and Letters Written from the Seat of War*. New York: G.P. Putnam's Sons, 1912.

United Daughters of the Confederacy. *South Carolina Women in the Confederacy*. Columbia, SC: The State Co., 1903.

Wallace, David D. *History of South Carolina*. 3 vols. New York: American Historical Society Inc., 1934.

———. *The Life of Henry Laurens*. New York: Knickerbocker Press, 1915.

Ward, Harry M. *George Washington's Enforcers: Policing the Continental Army*. Carbondale: Southern Illinois University Press, 2006.

Warner, Robert James. *Damn Slavers! A History of the Sea, Lake, and River Battles of the Civil War*. Bloomington, IN: AuthorHouse, 2006.

Webber, Mabel Louise, ed. "Order Book of John Faucheraud Grimké." *South Carolina Historical and Genealogical Magazine* 17 (1916): 116–20.

Wees, Hans van. *Status Warriors: War, Violence and Society in Homer and History*. Amsterdam, NL: Gieben, 1992.

Weintraub, Stanley. *Iron Tears: Rebellion in America, 1775–1783*. London: Simon & Schuster, 2005.

Wells, Edward L. *A Sketch of the Charleston Light Dragoons, from the Earliest Formation of the Corps*. Charleston, SC: Lucas, Richardson, 1888.

West Point Rice Mill Co. "West Point Rice Mill Records, 1860–1925." Charleston: (1201.00) South Carolina Historical Society.

Whilden, Mary S. *Recollections of the War, 1861–1865*. Columbia, SC: The State Co., 1911.

Wilkinson, Eliza. *Letters of Eliza Wilkinson, During the Invasion and Possession of Charlestown, S.C. by the British in the Revolutionary War*. Edited by Caroline H. Gilman. New York: Samuel Coleman, 1839.

Wilson, James Grant, T.M. Coan and A.N. Blakeman. *Personal Recollections of the War of the Rebellion*. New York: Knickerbocker Press, 1897.

Winthrop, William. *Military Law and Precedents*. Vol. 2. Boston: Little, Brown and Company, 1896.

Wise, Stephen R. *Lifeline of the Confederacy: Blockade Running During the Civil War*. Columbia: University of South Carolina Press, 1988.

Woodmason, Charles. *The Carolina Backcountry on the Eve of the Revolution*. Chapel Hill: University of North Carolina Press, 1953.

Wray, George. Papers. William L. Clements Library, University of Michigan, Ann Arbor.

Zierden, Martha, Steven D. Smith and Ronald W. Anthony. "Our Duty Was Quite Arduous": History and Archaeology of the Civil War on Little Folly Island, South Carolina. *Charleston Museum Leaflet* 32, Charleston, SC: Charleston Museum, 1995.

INDEX

A

Aiken 67
Aiken-Rhett House 132
alcohol 76
  ale 77
  brandy 77
  Madeira 50, 77, 78, 79, 138
  whiskey 77
  wine 77, 78, 91, 138
Anderson, Major Robert 121
André, Major John 79
Apprentices' Library Society 86
Arbuthnot, Admiral Mariot 20
arson 106
artisans 25, 26, 30
Asbury, Bishop Francis 31
Ashley River 58, 116, 125
Audubon, John James 67
Augusta 50, 64
Averill, Colonel J.H. 88

B

Bachman, John 67
Bailey, Godard 69

Baker, Amy Legare 22, 23
Baker, John 22
Ball, Charlotte 127
Ball, Keating 125, 126, 127, 128
Baltimore 27
Barton, Clara 72
Battery Wagner 105
Beauregard, General Pierre G.T. 45,
    47, 49, 72, 91, 96
beds 75, 84, 102, 115
Bennett, Colonel A.G. 53
Bennett's Rice Mill 80
Black, Dorothea deLiesseline 130
Black, Thomas 130
Blaine, Frank 11, 15
Blake, Governor Joseph 85
blockade runners 91, 94
Blue, Donald I. 118
Bluffton 47
Bonaparte, Napoleon 16
books 15, 23, 30, 50, 86, 87, 112, 135
Boston 25, 33, 130
box tombs 111, 112
Brabant plantation 115, 116

Brewton, Miles (goldsmith) 124, 128
Brewton, Miles (merchant) 31
Broad Street 97, 109
Bull, Lieutenant Governor William 110
bummers 81
bushwhackers 74
Butler, General Benjamin 130

C

Calhoun, Andrew 47
Calhoun, John C. 23, 47, 48
Calhoun Street 23
Camden 33, 38, 62, 117, 118
Canada 38
Cantey's plantation 81
Carolina Art Association 86
Catesby, Mark 67
Cathedral of St. John and St. Finbar 106
Central Park Zoo 76
ceramics 23, 30, 87, 91
  Chinese export porcelain 23
  porcelain 67
Chambersburg 19
Charleston Courier 96
Charleston Daily Courier 44, 105
Charleston Daily News 33, 98, 129, 130, 135
Charleston Light Dragoons 81
Charleston Mercury 19, 42, 44
Chattanooga 44
Cheraw 117
Chesapeake 25
Chesney, Alexander 75
Chestnut, Mary Boykin 58, 91
Childsbury 124
Christ Church (Mount Pleasant) 105, 112
Christ Church (Rutledge Avenue) 11
church bells 23, 105, 109
Church of England 104
Church of the Holy Communion 112

cigars 91
Circular Congregational Church 106
Clancy, W.D. 76
Clinton, General Sir Henry 28, 30, 31, 38, 39, 72
Coe, Edmund 11
Cold Harbor 130
Colleton, John 38
Columbia 16, 33, 48, 49, 50, 51, 62, 67, 81, 82, 109, 118
Columbia Phoenix 16, 50
Combahee River 28
Coming, John 125
Comingtee
  plantation 124, 125, 126, 127, 128
  rice mill 124, 126, 127, 128
communion tokens 117
Company K, Fourth South Carolina Cavalry 62
Congress, U.S. 14, 56, 74
Conyngham, Captain David P. 15
Cooper, Lord Anthony Ashley 27
Cooper River 65, 105, 124, 125
Coosawhatchie River 110
Cornwallis, General Charles 115
cotton 96
Cramer, Adolph 96

D

Daily Phoenix 33
Darby plantation 67
Davis, Colonel C.W.H. 14
Deas, John 69, 70
deLiesseline, Anne 130, 131
deLiesseline, Francis Gottier 130, 131
Deveaux, Major Andrew, Jr. 110, 111
Dill, Joseph 58, 60
Dill's Bluff plantation 58
Dill, Susannah 60
distemper 85
Donaldson, James 20
Downs, Joseph 26, 27

Doyle, Colonel 69
Drayton Hall 112

E

Early, General Jubal A. 19
earthquake of 1886 87, 88
Edgefield 67
Edisto Island 39, 64, 75, 84, 130
Elizabeth Street 132
Episcopal Diocese 112
Eutaw plantation 60
Eutaw Springs 74
Ewald, Johann von 21
Ewan, John 11

F

Federal blockade 91
Ferguson, Thomas P. 79, 80
Fifth Avenue Auction Rooms 102
Fifty-sixth New York Regiment 76
fine art 15, 16, 30, 50, 79, 84, 87, 88,
    130, 134
  paintings 16, 102, 132, 133, 134, 135
  portraits 67, 130, 131, 132
  statuary 16
fires 19, 85, 97
  fire of 1778 86
  fire of 1861 49, 86, 106
firewood 75, 105, 106
First (Scots) Presbyterian 117, 118
Fisher, Eliza Middleton 134
foraging 64, 71, 72, 73, 75, 76, 77,
    79, 80, 81, 82, 83, 84
forts
  Granby 89
  Johnson 58, 60
  Sullivan 36, 113
  Sumter 56
  Ticonderoga 127
Fourth Regiment South Carolina
    Volunteers 44
Freedmen's Bureau 84

French Huguenot Church 48, 117, 131
Friday 126
furniture 15, 16, 19, 21, 26, 30, 35,
    50, 56, 64, 75, 79, 87, 88, 91,
    100, 102, 110, 115, 132, 135

G

Gaillard, Peter Charles 130, 131, 132
Gates, General Horatio 38
Gelzer, Susan 91
Genghis Khan 14
George II 115
George III 36, 111
Gettysburg 44, 45
Gillman, Reverend Samuel 105
Gillmore, General Quincy A. 16, 47,
    49, 72
Glen, Governor James 87
gold 17, 19, 27, 33, 50, 69, 91, 129, 135
Goose Creek 56, 105
Gourdin, Robert N. 47, 48
Gowrie plantation 64, 65
Grace (New York) 129
Grant, General Ulysses S. 50
grist 84
Guerard, Benjamin 122
gunboat fairs 91

H

Hamilton, Paul 39, 42
Hampton's Legion 83
Hampton, Wade, I 88
Hampton, Wade, III 82, 83
Harrison, Joseph 42
Harvard University 135
Hatch, General John P. 16, 80
Haw's Shop 81
Henderson, Colonel William 88
Hessians 21, 23, 28, 58, 60
Heyward, Nathaniel 28, 77
Hilton Head Island 64
Hinson, William Godber 138

Holmes, Francis Simmons 67
Holst, Charles 49, 94
Horlbeck, Edward 62, 64
Huger, Benjamin 16
Hugo, Victor 14
Huguenots 77
hurricanes 85, 86, 87
  hurricane of 1752 87
  hurricane of 1838 87

I

Indigo 25
Isaiah 14

J

James Island 22, 36, 39, 58, 96, 107,
    109, 117, 138
Jeffords, Mrs. William 60, 62
jewelry 17, 23, 33, 36, 50, 56, 62,
    67, 84
John Street 96
Judd, Emma 18, 19

K

Keir, Mrs. 36
King, Milo 127
Kirk, Martha L.E. 130, 132

L

Laurens, Henry 58, 123, 124
Law of Nations 72
Lee, Colonel Henry 74, 89
Lee, General Robert E. 44
Legare, Thomas 23
Lemprière's Point 23
Lewis and Clark 67
Lewis, Lieutenant Richard 44
Lexington County 88
Lincoln, Abraham 42, 121
Lincoln, General Benjamin 48, 88, 89

livestock 28, 75, 76, 79, 110
London 30, 36, 124
London Chronicle 36
Lorentz, Richard 36
Lowndes, Rawlins 69
Lowndes, Sarah 69
Loyalists 19, 28, 36, 38, 39, 42, 75
Lucas, Jonathan 77
Lynch, Thomas 44

M

Macbeth, Henrietta Gourdin Ravenel
    53, 56, 58, 69
Macbeth, Mayor Charles 53, 56
MacCusker, John J. 25
Macy, William L. 14
Manigault
  Alfred 62, 97
  Charles 77, 78, 87, 132, 135
  Charlotte Morris 129, 130, 132
  Gabriel 64, 78
  Henry Heyward 129
  Louis 62, 64, 65, 67, 77, 97, 132
Manning, William 124
Marcy, Dr. Henry 132, 133, 134, 135
Marion, General Francis 38, 111, 112
Marquin, Jonathon 20
Matadequin Creek 81
Mauder 115, 116
Maxwell, Major Andrew 89
Mazyck, William 86
McArty, Bonnie 11
McDonald, Theresa A. 91
McDuffie, Governor George 43
McLaurin, Catherine 75
McPhersonville 110
Meeting Street 96, 109
Mepkin plantation 58
merchants 25, 30
Metropolitan Museum of Art 26
Mexican-American War 81

Middleton
  Arthur 75
  Edward 134
  Henry 28
  Williams 75, 76, 100, 112, 134,
      135, 146, 147, 149
Middleton Place 75, 76, 112, 134
Montreat 119
Morris, Charles 129
Morris Island 19, 45, 91, 109
Motte, Colonel Isaac 58
Motte, Rebecca 31
Moultrie, General William 26, 73
Mount Pleasant Presbyterian 105
Mulberry plantation 69
Munro, James 86
Myers, Thomas J. 33, 34

N

Nashville 34
natural disasters 26
Nelson's Ferry 38
New Orleans 91, 130
New Town Creek 58
New York 76, 102, 127, 129, 132
Nichols, Major George 51, 81
Northeastern Railroad depot 96
northern aggression 20, 98
nullification 32, 47

O

Old Testament 14
127th New York Volunteers 31
Orangeburg 74
Order No. 7 16

P

Parker, Commodore Peter 36
Parliament 124
Parnassus plantation 56
Philadelphia 25, 77

Philipsburg Proclamation 28
Pitt, William 109
planters 25, 28, 30, 84
Pocotaligo River 105
Ponpon River 75
Porter, Reverend Anthony Toomer
      49, 112
Port Royal 17, 44, 64, 84, 110
Potter, Dr. Henry C. 129, 130
Powder Magazine 77, 78
Presbyterian Historical Foundation 119
Prevost, General Augustine 42
Prince George's 106
Prince William's Parish 110
Pringle, Jane Lynch 76

R

Ramsay, Dr. David 15, 84, 87
Ransom, Major General Robert 49
Rawdon, Lord 75
Reconstruction 100
Rhett, Henrietta Aiken 132
rice 23, 25, 27, 28, 65, 69, 75, 80, 84
Richard II 72
Rogers, John 99
Rutledge, Edward 122
Rutledge, Governor John 39

S

Saunders, Dr. Thomas J. 121
Savannah 42, 49, 65
Savannah River 103
Schimmelfennig, General Alexander 31
secession 28, 33, 42, 43, 56, 86
Second Presbyterian 117
Seventeenth Indiana Infantry 34
Shakespeare, William 14, 34
Sheldon
  church 110, 111, 112
  plantation 110

Sherman, General William T. 15, 16, 33, 34, 42, 48, 49, 50, 51, 53, 74, 75, 81, 82, 83, 104, 112, 121, 132
Shiloh 91
silk 18, 91
Silk Hope plantation 65
silver 11, 15, 16, 17, 23, 30, 33, 36, 50, 56, 58, 60, 62, 65, 67, 79, 87, 91, 109, 110, 112, 115, 116, 117, 118, 124, 125, 126, 127, 128, 129, 132
Simms, William Gilmore 48
Simonton, Charles H. 132
slaves 21, 23, 28, 31, 39, 110, 126
smallpox 85
Smith, Bishop Robert 104, 113, 115
South Carolina Gazette 86, 87, 110
South Carolina Weekly Gazette 74
Sprunt, Reverend Alexander 119
St. Andrew's 112, 116
Stewart, Colonel Alexander 56
St. George's Dorchester 105
St. James' Goose Creek 105
St. John's Berkeley 106
St. John's Colleton 105, 117
St. John's Episcopal (Winnsboro) 62
St. Mark's 106
St. Michael's 23, 109
Stoney Creek Presbyterian 105
Stono River 58
St. Paul's Goose Creek 105
St. Philip's 47, 48, 104, 113, 115, 117
Strawberry Chapel 124, 125, 126, 127, 128, 129
St. Stephens's 106
Sullivan, Grover 127
Sullivan, Martha 124, 127, 128
Sullivan's Island 87
Sumter County 75
Sumter, General Thomas 88

T

Tarleton, Sir Banastre 38
Temple of Bacchus 86
Tennant, William 104
Tennent, Mary Fripp 56, 58
Tennent, William 56, 58
tobacco 25, 60
Tolstoy, Leo 14
Tories 73, 75, 110, 111
Trapier, Reverend Paul 16, 62, 135
Treaty of Paris 124
Trenholm, George A. 67
Trevilian Station 81
Twain, Mark 31
Twenty-first Illinois Regiment 60
Twenty-first Massachusetts Colored Regiment 106
Twenty-first U.S. Colored Troops 31, 53
Twenty-seventh South Carolina Infantry 130
Tybee Island 110

U

Unitarian Church 105

V

Vattel, Emer de 72
Vicksburg 45

W

Wadmalaw Island 84
wagon trains 74, 75
Wantoot plantation 53, 56
water buffalo 75, 76
Watson, Colonel 69
Welsman, Captain James 48
West Indies 110
West Point rice mill 84
Whilden, Mary 17, 19, 44, 60

Whitehall 36
Wilkinson, Eliza 35, 36, 38, 75, 135
Williamsburg Antiques Forum 27
Winnsboro 62
Wood, Isaac 89
Woodword, Dr. Henry 27

Y

Yorktown 23

About the Author

J. Grahame Long is the chief curator for the Charleston Museum. He has published numerous articles on local history and antiques and served as an historical analyst for varied television and radio outlets. His first book, *Dueling in Charleston: Violence Refined in the Holy City* (The History Press, 2012), was a 2013 selection for the Piccolo Spoleto Literary Festival. A graduate of Presbyterian College, Long is married to Reverend Lissa Long and has two daughters. He and his family split their time between Charleston and Edisto Island.